THE DYNAMIC INFANT

Activities to enhance infant and toddler development

THE DYNAMIC INFANT

Activities to enhance infant and toddler development

REBECCA ANNE BAILEY, Ph.D.

Assistant Professor, Early Childhood Education
University of Central Florida
Orlando, Florida

ELSIE CARTER BURTON, Ph.D.

Professor, Department of Movement Science and
Physical Education, Florida State University,
Tallahassee, Florida

With 109 illustrations

Toys 'n Things Press

St. Paul, Minnesota

Originally published 1982 by The C.V. Mosby Company under the title The Dynamic Self.

ISBN: 0-934140-55-3   89-5012

Published by: Toys 'n Things Press
                   a division of Resources for Child Caring, Inc.
                   450 North Syndicate, Suite 5
                   St. Paul, Minnesota 55104

Distributed by: Gryphon House
                   PO Box 275
                   Mt. Rainier, MD 20712

                   Acropolis Books Ltd.
                   2400 17th Street NW
                   Wasington, DC 20009

Bailey, Rebecca Anne, 1952-
    The dynamic infant.

    Reprint. Originally published: Dynamic
self. St. Louis : Mosby, 1982.
    Bibliography: p.
    Includes index.
    1. Infants—Development. 2. Day care cen-
ters—Activity programs. 3. Toddlers. I. Burton,
Elsie Carter. II. Title.
HQ774.B28 1989   649'.5   89-5012
ISBN: 0-934140-55-3

Printed in the United States of America.

Preface

This book is written for fathers, mothers, grandparents, caregivers, child development specialists, baby-sitters, and day care center personnel. It is also written to serve as a text in courses dealing with child development. In other words, it is written for anyone who is interested in knowing about infants.

The title *The Dynamic Infant* reflects both the theme of the book and our purpose in writing it. We view young children as active agents in their own development. We believe that what children learn, how they learn it, how they feel about learning it, and what they feel about themselves and others are all vital concerns. Further, we believe that all of these factors interact in the learning process. We have therefore attempted to address them in the manner in which they interact.

The first two chapters of the book were developed to assist the reader in understanding the role of physical activity in the development of the "self." Emphasis is placed on the fact that infants are not only developing motor skills, they are also developing a sense of self and of their relationships with other people and the physical world.

Chapters 3 and 4 focus on the caregiver's interaction with the child and the relationship between the two of them. The four types of roles the caregiver must assume in the learning situation are explained. The relationship between the primary caregiver and the infant is described as being that of friends, with the basis of this relationship being mutual trust.

Chapters 5 and 6 are concerned with physical activities to enhance infant development. In Chapter 5, emphasis is placed on the role of movement in the infant's construction of reality. The suggested activities are designed to assist the infant in experiencing the reality of objects, spaces, time and cause-and-effect relationships. Chapter 6 focuses on activities to develop the infant's movement vocabulary. This vocabulary is both verbal and nonverbal. The nonverbal aspect consists of locomotor, nonlocomotor, and manipulative skills. The verbal aspect includes body and spatial awareness and concepts involving time and spatial relationships.

The final chapter deals with creating a play environment that stimulates learning. Various play objects and structures are described.

Throughout the book, we have attempted to stimulate a way of thinking about infant development that will enable readers to build their own frame of reference. We have sought to provide tools rather than rules and ideas rather than formulas. We encourage readers to release their creative ability so that they can discover and reveal their dynamic selves as they interact with infants.

Women's liberation has changed many areas of society, not the least of which is the written word. Many writers no longer use the pronoun *he*, but have instead shifted to the plural form *they*. Because we want to encourage the individuality of each infant, we have resisted this trend except in general statements about infants as a group. We prefer to retain the more personal tone of *he* and *she* in activities and stories relating to individual children. Therefore we have alternated between masculine and feminine pronouns in certain areas of the book. We hope this seems fair and nonsexist to the reader.

So many people have contributed to our learning that it would be impossible to acknowledge them all. We have learned from our parents' and teachers' interactions with us. But we have learned even more from children. By interacting with them, we became aware of their right to develop unique selves and of the vital role of movement in this process. Our concern for them kept us on task until our vision became the reality of this book.

The production of this book would have been impossible without the encouragement and assistance of many people. We wish to express our gratitude to Mickey Adair for providing his excellent photographs and to Christin for assisting us with the drawings. We wish to thank Pam Phelps for making available to us the children and facilities of her preschool center. Appreciation is gratefully acknowledged to the publisher's reviewers: Dr. Marjorie H. Friedburg and Dr. Edward G. Ponder, both at New York University, and to Patricia M. Straub and Ruth K. Kranzler, both at South Dakota State University. Finally, we wish to thank Dodie Zeiler who critically reviewed the manuscript and pointed out ways to make the text clearer and more useful.

Rebecca Anne Bailey
Elsie Carter Burton

Contents

THE DYNAMIC INFANT
Activities to enhance infant and toddler development

CHAPTER 1

The beginning

"Today I felt the baby move!" This statement (usually spoken with an air of excitement) expresses the mother's awareness of the baby as a dynamic (moving) being. We chose the "dynamic self" as the theme for this book because it encompasses the idea of the infant moving to discover and to develop. The term *dynamic* refers to energy, force, and action. The word *self* denotes the whole child. By using these two words together, we are implying that the movement activities of energetic infants are the means whereby they develop into fully functioning individuals.

The infant's first movements are *reflexes*. Reflexes are movements that occur automatically without having to be learned. These reflexive responses ensure that the infant will move in the way that is essential for survival. Thus from the very beginning, movement is the infant's vital link with life.

MOVEMENT AND LEARNING

Whenever babies move any part of their bodies, the potential exists for two kinds of learning to occur: learning to move and learning by moving. Learning to move involves the emergence and refinement of movement skills and the development of general movement abilities (Chapter 2). Learning by moving consists of infants forming associations and making cognitive relationships. This is the process whereby they gradually construct their reality.

As soon as infants become capable of forming mental images, they enter a new phase of self-development. From this point on, infants' experiences become symbolized and they translate these into awareness. Infants learn from transforming the messages in sensory stimulation into symbols. In other words, infants' awarenesses are the product of their learning.

Throughout this book we will emphasize the importance of the baby's early experiences with the primary caregiver. So let's use the following situation as an example. Let's say that the baby's mother walks up to the crib, bends over, smiles, and coos. This stimulates both visual and auditory senses in the infant. The baby sees the smiling face and hears the pleasant-sounding voice. The baby translates these messages into mental images. The infant then becomes aware by joining these images together. We call this process *forming associations* because it involves linking together similar messages.

Let's return to the example to see how the baby becomes aware of the mother's attention. We described how the sensory stimulation of seeing and hearing was translated into mental images. At first these are just meaningless sights and sounds. But the nerve cells in the newborn's brain are rapidly developing and soon she becomes capable of forming an association between the sensory stimulation and its source. Now the baby associates the pleasant sight and sound with a person. And very soon she will progress to associating the stimulation with a *particular* person. This is when the infant begins to form an attachment to the primary caregiver. The infant's ability to form associations serves as the basis for forming relationships. Being able to form an association between mental images is prerequisite to making a causal connection between them. The first step in becoming aware is being able to link two images together (associating them). The next step is being able to recognize how they fit together (relating them).

Fig. 1-1. Forming an attachment is the basis for forming relationships. Building a lasting relationship is essential for development.

Returning to the example, we can now describe how the infant's attachment to the mother is formed. The infant associates messages concerning pleasant sensory stimulation with the actions of a particular person. The baby makes these associations over and over as the mother repeats the activities that reflect concerned care. In time, the baby begins to relate the messages of pleasant sensations with the actions of this particular person. The baby has now learned that the mother provides comfort and removes discomfort, and this is the foundation on which their lasting relationship is built.

THE INFANT'S REALITY

Newborn infants' responses to the world are generalized and undifferentiated; that is, they cannot distinguish the difference between themselves

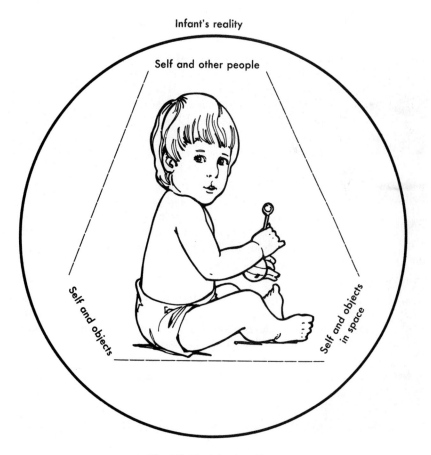

Fig. 1-2. The infant's reality.

and things that are not a part of them. Thus for several weeks after birth they simply respond reflexively to incoming sensory stimulation. Gradually their sense modalities and their nervous and muscular systems mature enough to enable them to distinguish the difference between "me" and "not me." This transition marks the beginning of self-awareness. In addition to the *self*, there are three other components of this reality: *self and other people*, *self and objects*, and *self and objects in space*. These components are arbitrary constructs, specified purely for purposes of discussion. The infant actually develops as a unified whole with all aspects of the self inter-related and developing simultaneously.

The development of self

The "self" is everything an individual is and does. An individual's thoughts, feelings, behaviors, and physical being, acting as an organized entity, all make up the self.

A baby lives in a continually changing world of experiences, and the center of this world is the dynamic self. By being dynamic the infant creates internal and external experiences. At first these experiences are purely sensory. But gradually the baby begins to reach out and purposefully manipulates some part of the environment. This is a sign that the baby is becoming aware that the self can affect the environment as well as that the environment can affect the self. Thus the self develops out of this interactive process between the infant and the environment. And although infancy is the most critical period of this development, it is an ongoing process that continues throughout the individual's entire lifetime.

Self and others

The single most important person in the infant's environment is the primary caregiver. This is the individual who will exert the most influence over the development of the self. As infants interact with the primary caregiver and other caregivers, their awareness of self-experiences is translated into a concept of self. Infants soon *learn* that certain behaviors cause people to respond to them in warm, accepting, and loving ways. Babies also *learn* that other kinds of behaviors cause people to become angry, disgusted, and rejecting. Because infants need to be accepted, they try to modify their behavior to obtain positive responses and to avoid negative ones. This is why it is vitally important for parents and other caregivers to be aware of infants' real needs. Babies need to be *unconditionally accepted* as themselves. Infants are never deliberately "bad." They just are! It is adults who place value-laden labels on infants' behaviors. We verbally and nonverbally convey our feelings to infants. Cooing, smiling, and playful reactions tell infants we accept and enjoy them. Actions such as frowning, a harsh tone of voice, or ignoring babies convey the message that we dislike and reject them. Infants internalize these responses and begin to see themselves reflected in

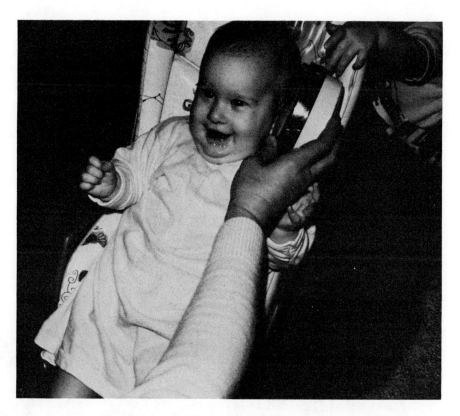

Fig. 1-3. Relating to objects provides exciting discoveries.

them. Thus their self-concepts are formed on the basis of how others perceive and respond to them.

There is another long-lasting result of the infant–primary caregiver relationship. It is generally accepted by developmental theorists that the bond between infant and mother (or primary caregiver) serves as the model for all other human relationships; this first relationship determines whether or not the infant will learn to form attachments with other human beings. The results of research studies indicate that certain factors influence the development of this relationship (Yarrow, Rubenstein, and Pedersen, 1975). The principal factors facilitating this development are as follows:

1. A stable caregiver who provides individualized attention
2. A caregiver who is responsive when the infant expresses distress as a result of a biological need, such as hunger or fatigue
3. High levels of stimulation provided by the caregiver

The factors specified in 2 and 3 are dealt with in more detail in Chapter 3. These factors are also emphasized elsewhere in the book in descriptions of movement activities.

Self and objects

Becoming adjusted to a new world consumes all of the newborn's energies. Infants' sensory capabilities and neuromuscular systems must continue to develop for several additional weeks before they will become capable of relating to their environment. However, by the time they are 4 months old, their neuromuscular systems are well enough developed to permit voluntary movement. At this age infants can usually control their eye movements, turn their heads, and hold them erect. They can also reach out to contact, grasp, and manipulate objects. During the next 4 months the babies' reality will enlarge to encompass the relationships between themselves and objects. The construction of this aspect of their reality is facilitated by the emergence of gross motor skills such as rolling over, sitting upright, and crawling.

Self and objects in space. Infants' dynamic selves are much more evident when they become capable of moving through space. Being able to voluntarily move from one location to another opens a whole new world to chil-

Fig. 1-4. The ability to move markedly enlarges the infant's world.

dren. They are no longer limited to exploration of the objects someone else provides. Now they can move through space and explore anything within reach. This budding ability can be a source of conflict if the parents overlook its importance. Some adults maintain that the baby must "learn to leave my things alone." People with this attitude fail to realize that the infant's natural inclination to explore everything within reach is developmentally necessary. An infant is not capable of distinguishing between objects that are "OK to touch" and those an adult has designated as being "off limits." This is the reason the baby's environment should be child proofed. Cherished and unsafe objects should simply be placed out of young children's reach. This leaves children free to explore everything in their world and stimulates natural curiosity and creativity.

As soon as infants can perceive the physical reality of their bodies, they also become capable of making spatial relationships. Examples of early spatial relationships are moving the feet upward so they can be grasped by the hands, bringing the hands together, and reaching for and grasping objects

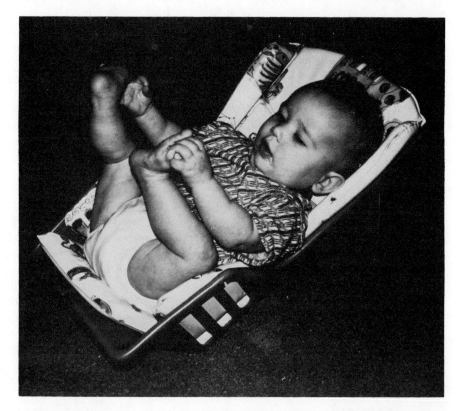

Fig. 1-5. Moving the feet upward so they can be grasped with the hands involves making spatial relationships.

in space. These activities show that the infant is developing depth perception. They also illustrate how the infant is gradually preparing for the challenges inherent in moving through space. In addition to being able to judge distances, the toddler must also be able to detect differences in height. Development of these abilities is accompanied by the beginning awareness of differences in the size and shape of people, objects, and spaces. The young child's world is now literally "taking shape." Each discovery becomes the means whereby the child forms new associations and makes new relationships. Thus reality is enlarged and at the same time it becomes more complex.

THE INFANT'S NEED TO MOVE

Babies are born with the natural urge to move in ways that will ensure their natural development. However, we cannot assure that the type of care they receive will permit the free expression of these natural urges. We live in a society that restricts rather than encourages freedom of movement. Babies are often restrained by tight-fitting clothing, by being strapped into infant seats, and by being penned up in small enclosures. Also, babies are frequently rewarded for inactivity rather than for being their natural, energetic selves. Obviously there are times when some limitations, routines, and behavioral expectations are necessary and desirable. However, these should be determined by the infant's development needs as well as by the caregiver's convenience.

The need of infants to move must be viewed in terms of their learning potential. To fully develop this potential, you must view the child's physical activities as having a purpose. Young children are never "just playing." Each action of infants in some way extends their development. Some of the infant's inherent abilities will emerge naturally. But as we have pointed out, it is unlikely that these abilities will reach their full potential unless the baby's daily activities are purposefully planned. But even more important, these activities must be shared with an enthusiastic and supportive adult. This is why we have not designed a "recipe book" that specifies the exact ingredients to be used or the prescribed way they are to be mixed. Rather we have attempted to create a "way of thinking" about the learning potential within the child's various movement experiences. We have then given examples of activities that will develop this potential. This approach is based on the assumption that if we can convey just enough information to get you started, you will experience enough excitement and satisfaction to keep you going. Then you and the child together can create additional learning activities to meet his individual developmental needs.

SUMMARY

The "dynamic self" was selected as the theme for this book because it emphasizes the importance of movement in the normal development of the total child. As young children participate in movement activities, they become more aware as well as more physically skilled. As the infant's development progresses, this awareness becomes the infant's reality. There are four components of this reality. These are self-awareness and awareness of self and others, self and objects, and self and objects in space.

Infants' natural desire to move is nature's way of ensuring their participation in developmentally essential physical activities. It is imperative for caregivers to recognize the necessity of providing a varied program of movement activities because these activities are infants' primary learning medium.

SUGGESTED READINGS

Caplan, F., and Caplan T. *The power of play*. New York: Anchor Press, 1973.

Frank, L.K. *On the importance of infancy*. New York: Random House, Inc., 1966.

Kaluger, G., and Kaluger, M.F. *Human development: the span of life* (2nd ed.). St. Louis: The C.V. Mosby Co., 1979.

McClinton, B.S., and Meier, B.G. *Beginnings: The psychology of early childhood*. St. Louis: The C.V. Mosby Co., 1978.

Robeck, M.C. *Infants and children: their development and learning*. New York: McGraw-Hill, Inc., 1978.

Sherrod, K., Vietze, P., and Friedman, S. *Infancy*. Monterey, Calif.: Brooks/Cole Publishing Co., 1978.

Yarrow, L.J., Rubenstein, J.L., and Pedersen, F.A. *Infant and environment: early cognitive and motivational development*. New York: John Wiley & Sons, Inc., 1975.

CHAPTER 2

Becoming a dynamic self

An infant is not born with a self. The self must develop. It is the product of learning: learning to perceive, learning to relate, and learning to move. All learning is initiated by sensory stimulation. Newborns respond to sensory stimulation by moving reflexively. These are called *involuntary* movements because they occur automatically. Newborns' nervous systems are not yet well enough developed to enable them to process information and respond *voluntarily*. However, this development does occur rapidly during the first few months as infants progress from purely reflexive movements to movements involving some voluntary control. We have named these first voluntary actions *control skills*. This term emphasizes the fact that infants can now exert some control over their own bodies as well as exert some control over some aspects of the environment.

CONTROL SKILLS

The control skills mark the beginning of the development of a dynamic self. As the infant gains more control over her own actions, she becomes free to explore herself and to relate this self to the world. The infant's exploration stimulates learning, and learning enables the infant to exert more control. And so the baby's development progresses from day to day with each new bit of learning increasing the potential for more learning. Soon the control skills become developed enough to enable the baby to voluntarily move through space and to freely manipulate objects. This transition makes it possible for the infant to eventually become a free and independent self.

The skills that enable infants to gain control over their bodies first appear as controlled movements of the head and neck, then the trunk, and finally the arms, legs, hands, and feet. This orderly sequence follows the *law of developmental direction*. This law states that development proceeds from head to tail (cephalocaudal), and from the trunk of the body to the extremities (proximodistal). This explains why infants first learn how to lift their heads and chests, then progress to sitting upright, and finally progress to standing. This law also explains why babies first gain control over the muscles of the trunk (the center of the body), followed by control of the arms and legs. (It also explains why preschool children should not not be expected to learn fine-motor skills such as handwriting.)

The skills that enable infants to begin gaining control of their environment are reaching, grasping, and releasing (dropping). These skills naturally emerge as infants gain control over their arms, hands, and fingers (the distal parts of the body). Maturation of the nerves and muscles that control the eyes is also a factor. Babies must be able to visually track the movements of the hands in relation to objects they are reaching toward and attempting to

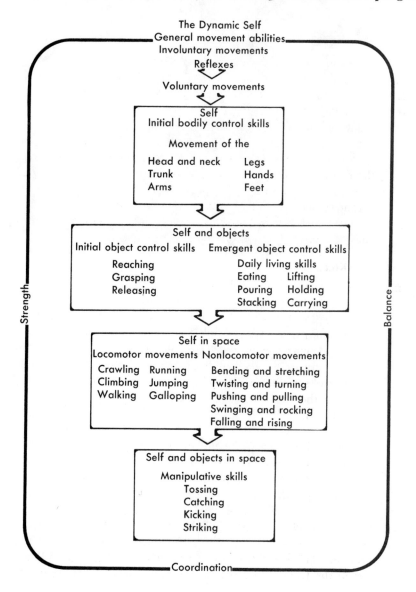

The Dynamic Self
General movement abilities
Involuntary movements
Reflexes

Voluntary movements

Self
Initial bodily control skills

Movement of the

Head and neck — Legs
Trunk — Hands
Arms — Feet

Self and objects

Initial object control skills — Emergent object control skills

Reaching — Daily living skills
Grasping — Eating — Lifting
Releasing — Pouring — Holding
Stacking — Carrying

Self in space

Locomotor movements — Nonlocomotor movements

Crawling — Running — Bending and stretching
Climbing — Jumping — Twisting and turning
Walking — Galloping — Pushing and pulling
Swinging and rocking
Falling and rising

Self and objects in space

Manipulative skills
Tossing
Catching
Kicking
Striking

Strength

Balance

Coordination

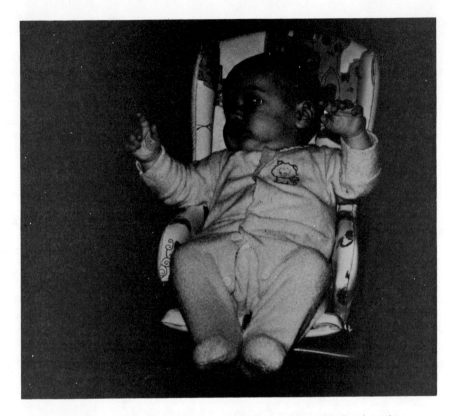

Fig. 2-1. The emergence of hand-eye coordination is evidenced by hand watching.

grasp. The learning that results from the infant practicing these early hand-eye coordination tasks establishes the foundation necessary for the emergence of more complex object control skills; that is, the initial skills of reaching, grasping, and releasing become more refined movement patterns. The skills that emerge as this refinement progresses enable infants to become somewhat self-directing. They begin to place food in their mouths, to pour liquids out of containers, to stack objects one on top of another, and to lift, hold, and carry objects. These emergent object control skills will in turn serve as the foundation for skills involving the control of the self and objects in space (the manipulative skills).

LOCOMOTOR SKILLS

To *locomote* means to move through space from one place to another. The infant's first locomotor movements are usually crawling patterns. The ability to crawl emerges as the baby gains control of the muscles in the head, neck, and trunk. Crawling also requires the infant to coordinate movement of the arms and legs.

Fig. 2-2. Climbing and crawling are similar movement patterns.

Climbing is a movement pattern similar to crawling. However, children frequently lead with one side of the body while climbing. For example, they will reach with the right hand, and then bring the right knee or foot upward. They will then bring the body parts on the left side of the body in line with the right side, but when they are ready to reach upward again, they will reach with the body parts on the right side. In time children learn how to coordinate movements of both sides of the body and will progress to leading alternately with the right and left sides.

Shortly after children master the control skill of standing upright, they usually progress to the skill of walking. Walking is actually a complex movement pattern. To walk, children must resist the force of gravity pulling them downward and at the same time maintain a balanced position on one foot while stepping forward with the other foot. They must also coordinate the movements of the right and left sides of the body to take steps. When a toddler begins to walk, he usually simplifies the task by holding onto something or someone. However, the toddler's desire for independence typically takes over before long and he strikes out alone. These initial attempts frequently result in a loss of balance, causing the toddler to fall down a lot. This is perfectly normal. The toddler is learning how to control himself in space and with the proper encouragement and practice he will soon be successful.

Learning to walk can be viewed as a transitional skill. Once children have learned how to walk, they soon progress to running, jumping, and galloping. All of these skills require the maintenance of a balanced, upright body position in combination with strength and coordination. Therefore when children have learned the basic lesson of controlling their bodies in space, they can rapidly progress to exerting this control in a variety of other ways.

NONLOCOMOTOR SKILLS

Newborn infants are capable of executing the nonlocomotor skills of bending, stretching, and twisting. The term *nonlocomotor* is used to refer to this classification of skills because a person does not move through space or from one place to another. Instead, a person moves different body parts or the body as a whole while remaining in the same location. For example, infants soon learn that they can pull things toward themselves and push them away. They also soon experience the joy of swinging their arms about in space. As soon as babies can sit up, they normally respond to rhythmic stimulation by rocking to and fro. When babies become toddlers, falling and rising become familiar movement patterns.

By practicing nonlocomotor skills, the child develops strength and coordination. With practice, these skills will continue to qualitatively develop

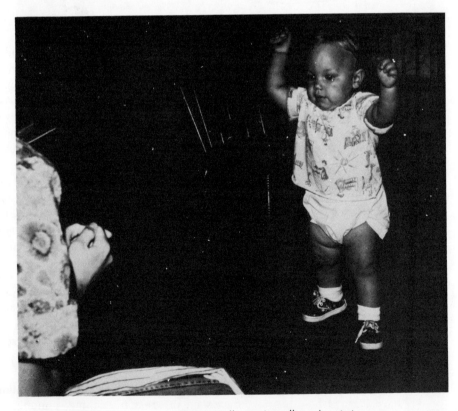

Fig. 2-3. It all begins with one small step. A small step is a start. . . .

throughout childhood and adolescence. They become the primary determinants of graceful and rhythmic body movements. This is why the development of these skills during infancy is vitally important.

MANIPULATIVE SKILLS

While toddlers are learning to control themselves in space, they are also learning how to control objects in space. Toddlers begin controlling objects in various ways, such as by tossing, catching, kicking, or striking. We call these manipulative skills because the children are manipulating objects. By relating to objects in space in this way, children not only develop skill, but also develop concepts by learning to detect differences in direction, level, size, and shape. They also begin to associate sizes and shapes with the names of certain objects. Finally, they make relationships between their own actions and the actions of different objects. And to think all of this is going on in the minds and bodies of such young children!

GENERAL MOVEMENT ABILITIES

At the same time children are developing specific kinds of movement patterns, they are also developing general movement abilities, which are necessary in the execution of all types of movement tasks.

The most basic general movement ability is *balance*. Toddlers must be able to maintain a balanced upright body position before they can execute any of the locomotor or manipulative skills. The ability to balance is largely dependent on the infant having developed sufficient *strength* to withstand the force of gravity. Strength is also essential in all lifting, carrying, pushing, pulling, climbing, and hanging activities. Therefore the development of strength becomes vitally important.

Coordination is also an essential prerequisite ability. The three aspects of coordination are general body coordination, hand-eye coordination, and foot-eye coordination. General body coordination develops according to the laws of developmental direction (p. 10). The baby's reaching and grasping develop hand-eye coordination, as does the baby's participation in manipulative skills, such as catching and striking. Foot-eye coordination results from the child contacting any kind of object with the foot. Examples of these kinds of activities are kicking at objects suspended above the bed or kicking at objects lying on the floor.

The development of these movement abilities is dependent on participation in a great deal of physical activity. Therefore throughout later sections of this book we will be emphasizing the importance of this development.

Fig. 2-4. The manipulative skills of, **A,** catching, **B,** kicking, and **C,** striking involve controlling objects in space.

SUMMARY

The development of a dynamic self proceeds in an orderly fashion. It begins with infants gaining control over their own bodies. This control is then extended to include the self and objects. At first infants execute initial object control skills. They then gradually become capable of executing more complex object control skills. These more complex skills emerge as daily living skills.

The development of the ability to control the self in relation to objects is parallel to the development of control of the self in space. Infants begin executing the nonlocomotor movements of bending, stretching, and twisting as soon as they are born. Other nonlocomotor movements emerge as strength and coordination increase. The development of the ability to control the body as it moves through space makes much more of the world accessible to the child. Also the ability to move about in an upright body position frees the hands and feet to handle and control objects in a much more versatile manner. This freedom of movement creates the opportunity for the child to develop the manipulative skills.

The development of all these physical skills is interwoven with the development of the general movement abilities. Balance, strength, and coordination are essential for skill development. These abilities continue to develop at the same time as the child is participating in activities requiring physical skill.

The development of the dynamic self is a complex process that is determined by maturation and learning. The infant gradually and sequentially progresses from involuntary reflexive movements to the development of complex skills involving the control of the self and objects in space.

SUGGESTED READINGS

Corbin, C.B., *A textbook of motor development* (2nd ed.). Dubuque, Iowa: Wm. C. Brown Co., Publishers, 1980.

Cratty, B.J. *Perceptual and motor development in infants and children* (2nd ed.). Englewood Cliffs, N.J.: Prentice-Hall, Inc., 1979.

Espenschade, A.S., and Eckert, H.M. *Motor development* (2nd ed.). Columbus, Ohio: Charles E. Merrill Publishing Co., 1980.

Musick, J.S., and Householder, J. *Infant development: from theory to practice.* Belmont, Calif.: Wadsworth Publishing Company, 1986.

Nelson, C. *Infant movement: normal and abnormal development.* Journal of Health, Physical Education, Recreation and Dance, September, 1988: 43-46.

Ridenour, M.V. (ed.). *Motor development: issues and applications.* Princeton, N.J.: Princeton Book Co., Publishers, 1978.

Zaichkowsky, L.D., Zaichkowsky, L.B., and Martinek, T.J. *Growth and development: the child and physical activity.* St. Louis: The C.V. Mosby Co., 1989.

CHAPTER 3

Interacting with young children

The fact that infancy is a period of rapid change is evident when you watch young children play. You can easily see how an activity that challenges a 12-month-old no longer holds the interest of an 18-month-old. You may also observe this same activity frustrating a 6-month-old who is not developmentally ready to master it. Children who are the same age also differ from each other. For this reason, it is best to avoid rigid comparisons between children or to textbook norms. Each child has developed a unique set of prerequisite abilities. These abilities determine how the child responds in specific activities, and it is these prerequisite abilities that determine her physical activity needs. Each child must begin at her own level on the developmental scale and progress from there. The problem is how to determine this level. You can do this by carefully observing her while she is playing and by experimenting with different types of activities. The child's responses will indicate which activities hold her interest and stimulate her exploration. These activities will then serve as a starting point, with the processes of observation and participation serving as guides for selecting future activities.

We have previously emphasized that each child is a unique individual and that there are ways in which each child differs from other children. Our goal must be to treat each child as a unique individual and to promote the optimal development of each child. As soon as children start school they will in all likelihood be subjected to crushing requirements for uniform group behavior and standardized achievement. Such expectations have no place in the lives of young children.

THE CAREGIVER'S ROLES

The caregiver must play four kinds of roles to maximize the learning potential within the play environment. These four roles are *supervisor*, *participant*, *facilitator*, and *observer*. These are not four entirely separate roles. They constantly overlap and intermingle, but the distinguishing factor is largely one of focus. As a supervisor, you focus on safety; as a participant, you focus on yourself; as a facilitator, you focus on the activity; and, as an observer, you focus on the child. It is unrealistic to assume that you can focus equally on safety, yourself, the activity and the child all at one time. No one can attend to everything that is happening. Therefore, you must decide which aspect is the primary concern at the moment and make that your priority.

Being a supervisor

Supervision is the most essential skill for any primary caregiver. Supervision equals safety and safety is a key factor in all healthy learning and development. One person must always be designated the supervisor. This person positions herself in the area of "highest risk" but also where she can see all the children. For example, if you have a climber in your room, the supervisor may position herself by the climber, but in view of the entire room. Some children that have not learned to control their aggressive impulses may create high risk areas wherever they play. In this case, the supervisor may float about the room following this particular child, yet be alert to the safety needs of other children. Other high risk areas may include: (1) an area of the room with new equipment or toys, (2) an area of the room containing limited numbers of popular toys, (3) an area of the room where high energy is generated (this will vary from day to day, moment to moment), (4) an area of the room overpopulated with children. Once the supervisor has located his position in the room, he must be alert to the need to change that position depending on the high risk needs created out of children's play choices. The supervisor has the responsibility of preventing dangerous situations and signaling other caregivers, who are in different roles (i.e., facilitator, participant, observer), to resolve any conflicts. It is crucial that the supervisor be the eyes and ears of the classroom rather than the "doer."

Children who attend early childhood educational programs may develop aggressive behaviors as a means of conflict resolution when there is a lack of adult supervision and guidance. Aggressive behaviors appear to be inborn forces with one common feature: they are an attempt to control and master ourselves within our environment. Children under three do not have the cognitive or verbal ability to express anger, fear, frustration or concern without adult guidance.[1] Because of inexperience and an imperfect understanding of consequences, all children need adult support and guidance to handle strong emotions. If left to handle these feelings and impulses unsupervised, violence upon one another results.

The number of available staff members will often dictate the role of the caregiver. If there is one adult for 15 children, the only role available is that of supervisor. If more staff members are available, a wider variety of caregiver roles can be employed to improve the program's quality.

---

[1] Blum, M. *The Day-Care Dilemma: Women and Children First.* Lexington, Massachusetts: Lexington Books D.C. Heath and Company, 1983.

Being a participant

Playing with a young child can be a most exhilarating experience. If you are a willing participant, the child's curiosity and delight will soon captivate you. And if you let yourself fully share in the child's fun and excitement, you will emerge from the experience with a renewed sense of life's pleasures. Sharing the child's natural playfulness offers you an opportunity to set aside the rigid, restrictive expectations inherent in adult behaviors and to get down on the floor and just get lost in the joy of play. The more you are able to "let go" and "have fun just being you," the more both you and the child will gain from the shared experiences. The ability to "let go" is supported by the fact that you know another caregiver is assigned to the role of supervisor.

As a participant, your primary focus will be on the way that you are interacting with the child in the activity. However, it is equally important that you function as a stimulator as well. This implies that you are constantly alert to ways the activity can be modified to provide new or additional stimulation. Modification of an activity comes from picking up the cues from the child and changing them slightly. For example, a child may be stacking cups, one within another, and you notice this in your play. You begin rolling the stacked cups like a log. The child may imitate you with delight and begin rolling the stack of cups. You can next roll the stack of cups toward another object and knock it over. The child will squeal with excitement and the play continues. Notice the play involves each participant taking turns and picking up cues from each other. This play is the foundation for sharing, cooperating and taking turns. It sets the stage for the development of communication skills that emerge later in life when more complex skills evolve. This "picking up on cues" form of stimulation is necessary in order to maintain your interest as well as the interest of the child. You must constantly be ready to answer the question, "where can we go from here?" This means you must be mentally as well as physically involved in the activity.

Spontaneity is one of the most important characteristics of a caregiver in the role of participant. When spontaneity is matched with insight, the caregiver can create an endless variety of stimulating learning activities. This is why it is so important for you to sense and respond to the child's needs. Flexibility is the key factor in maintaining your interest as well as that of the child.

It is vital that all of your interactions with the child reflect how you really feel. So, if you don't *feel* like participating in an activity, *don't do it*. You may be tired, worried or preoccupied, or you may simply not enjoy or feel comfortable doing a certain activity. Then don't do it! You must not force yourself to do an activity any more than you would push the child to engage in activities he won't enjoy. If your relationship with a child is characterized by honesty, fairness, and a concern for each other's needs and feelings, this will not be a problem.

When you choose to participate with the child, both you and the child will have a good time. We all learn more of what really matters when we enjoy what we are doing. But, even more importantly, when learning is fun, the child will come to think of learning activities as enjoyable experiences. He will enthusiastically anticipate these kind of pleasurable moments. The choice is yours. Potentially exciting activities can become drudgery if you insist on conducting them as stiff, adult-directed training procedures. In contrast, you can take a very ordinary, routine task and make it fun if you are enthusiastic and use a relaxed approach. We do want to re-emphasize, however, that your enthusiasm and enjoyment must be genuine. Remember, if you need a model, watch the child!

Being a facilitator

As a facilitator, you will be focusing on the activity—the learning process itself. You will be more effective if you are familiar with some of the factors that influence the learning process. Children learn more easily when new material is similar to what they already know and understand. The reason for this resides in the basic mode of development that characterizes all living creatures. Development occurs through a process of active adaptation to the surrounding environment. The process consists of two interrelated functions: *assimilation* and *accommodation.** Assimilation is the process whereby the messages contained in sensory stimulation are taken in, filtered through and made to fit with what children already know. Children then accommodate (alter slightly) their way of thinking, feeling, talking or moving to adjust to the new input. For children to be able to learn something new quickly, the new input (information, skill, feeling, or attitude) must closely resemble something familiar.

Sometimes it is necessary to introduce children to something new that is markedly different from the familiar. When these situations arise, children need you to assist them in two ways: they need you to help bridge the gap between the new and the familiar, and they need your assistance in developing their own ways of searching for answers. In all situations children need to be encouraged to become self-directed learners. Whenever possible, help them to develop problem-solving skills and to discover their own answers. All too often, we think of ourselves as dispensers of facts. We see ourselves as possessing the necessary knowledge and envision our role as being the source of the child's information. In this mode we focus on literal information. What color is it? Is it hard or soft? What day is it? Is it the same or different? Certainly there is some knowledge we as facilitators can dispense; however, there are also ways of knowing that the child must discover. To facilitate this discovery, we focus on the child's learning process rather than the product. We ask questions such

---

*These terms were coined by Piaget and are explained in many of the references to his work.

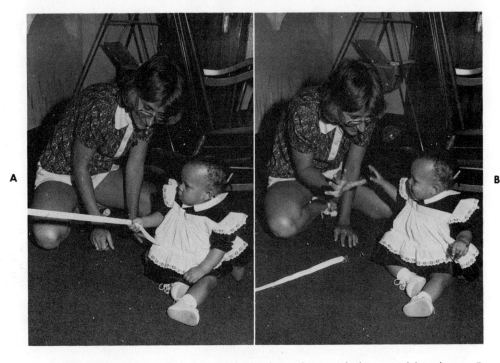

Fig. 3-1. A, Adults can help the infant bridge the gap between the known and the unknown. **B,** The experience of "letting go" enables the child to observe cause and effect.

as: What else could you do? What would happen if...? How else could you...? What caused that to happen? What do you think will happen to it? Have you tried...? By asking these questions we are saying to the child, "I value your discovery process." Young children must not be expected to verbally answer these questions. However, asking children these questions stretches their adaptation process and promotes further exploration.

Being an observer

Observing may be defined as interpreting what one sees and hears. We are constantly observing whether we are aware of it or not. Most of our observations concern our physical surroundings or other people. We may, for example, look at our environment and note things that need to be done, such as cleaning the house, raking the yard, or repairing the fence. Or we may notice things that give us pleasure, such as a sunset, flowers blooming, or the clean appearance of a freshly mopped floor. When we observe people, we may focus on their physical appearance, their actions, or the manner in which they interact with each other. We may also observe these same things about ourselves. We may look in a mirror and check our appearance; we may closely attend to a task we are performing with our hands; or we may take note of what we are saying to another person and how they are responding. These examples illustrate the fact that observation is an essential aspect of our everyday lives. We become aware of the things we observe and we overlook the things we fail to observe. This is why observation is such an important part of your interaction with the child.

In your role as an observer, you will be focusing on the child's behavior. There are two kinds of behavior: overt and covert. Overt behavior is what the child is doing or how she is physically responding. Covert behavior is the child's internal feelings and thoughts. We cannot see a child's covert behavior, but we can make assumptions about it on the basis of what we do see and hear. Young children often physically express their thoughts and feelings. A keen observer knows how to interpret what the child is saying verbally and nonverbally. For example, when the baby cries, it is usually a sign that he is feeling some physical or emotional discomfort. The caregiver attempts to determine the cause of the discomfort by observing the baby's physical condition and her behavior. Causes that are physically evident (such as the baby having a wet diaper) are easy to detect. However, when the cause is a feeling, it is much more difficult to determine. The baby may be feeling tired, hungry, ill or lonely. You must be able to accurately interpret what you observe in order to make a decision concerning the appropriate action.

How to observe. The process of observing consists of the following steps:

Observe → Evaluate → Make a decision

The first step in this process involves watching and listening. Caregivers must attend to what infants are doing as well as to the sounds they are making. This means attending to whole body action, to movements of body parts, to facial expressions, and to all of the audible expressions. Observing is an active process and the observer must be mentally alert and continuously attentive.

We wish to emphasize that there is a clear distinction between observing and supervising. In the role of supervisor, the adult is looking at the contextual situations that may lead to danger, whereas the observer is concentrating on a child's behavior.

Observing is also an ongoing process, and the observer must attend to the entire series of ongoing behaviors as well as to the particular behaviors within the series. Part of the message inherent in a child's behavior is contained in the continuity of his or her actions.

An observer must be both selective and objective. You cannot possibly focus on everything that is going on at one time. Being selective involves deciding beforehand what you will attempt to detect. We can compare this to going shopping. You must decide before you leave the house what it is that you desire to buy; whether it is groceries, clothing, toys, or furniture. You then select the store where you can obtain the type of merchandise you need. When you get to the store, you select particular items. The same kind of procedures are followed when observing infants.

The following examples illustrate some of the behaviors you may want to observe.

1. What whole body movements does the infant execute?
   - Rolls over
   - Lifts the head and chest
   - Crawls
   - Walks
   - Stands

2. What types of reaching movements does the infant make?
   - Swats at objects
   - Extends arm(s) toward object
   - Flails arms
   - Reaches directly toward object

3. What types of visual focusing and tracking does the infant display?
   - Follows a moving object
   - Appears to enjoy bright colors and pictures
   - Watches you as you move around the room

4. What kind of interest does the infant demonstrate relative to toys?
   - Reaches toward moving objects
   - Holds objects placed in the hands
   - Picks up objects

5. How does the infant respond to different voice tones?
   - Singing
   - Conversation
   - High pitch
   - Strong reprimand
   - Low pitch

6. How does the child demonstrate wanting something?
   - Points
   - Cries
   - Grabs your hand
   - Takes you to the object desired

7. How does the child respond to frustration?
   - Cries
   - Leaves task and moves to a new task
   - Gets angry
   - Seeks assistance

These examples illustrate the kinds of overt behaviors you can observe. As you work with a particular child and become more familiar with his movement abilities and developmental needs, you can be much more selective. You may decide to focus on the quality of a movement pattern and the behaviors the infant displays while practicing it. For example, when a child begins to walk, you would observe how he executes the walking pattern. You would notice how often he tumbles down, how he reacts to this, how readily he tries again, how many steps he can take and how often he reverts to crawling. As you become a more practiced observer, you will find you tend to be more selective simply because you are not as distracted by irrelevant factors.

While your ability to be selective affects the quality of your observations, your ability to be objective will also affect that quality. Being objective means being able to see beyond the cuteness of a child's behavior. Adults tend to be captivated by an infant's charm and playful nature. Of course, these feelings are important factors in the adult-child relationship, but they can be very real deterrents to objectivity. When you are functioning in the role of observer, you must try to put aside your emotional attachment to the child and gather the kinds of information that will enable you to evaluate his development and make decisions concerning his developmental needs.

Evaluation. The second step in the process of observing an infant's movement behaviors is your evaluation. This will be more accurate and useful if you develop the ability to be a systematic observer. Being systematic means scanning the play environment and taking note of all the factors that are influencing the child's actions. In other words, you move beyond determining what the child is doing to why he is doing it. Three kinds of things may be relevant aspects of the child's play environment:

Fig. 3-2. The captivating charm of a "dynamic infant"

1. Physical surroundings—whether the child is indoors or out, the location of furniture or other structures, the weather and temperature, the playing surface (grass, concrete, wood, carpet)
2. Available play objects
3. Other people—the caregiver, other familiar adults, other children, strangers

As you scan the child's environment, you must note the nature of these factors and then evaluate whether or not they are having an effect on the way the child is playing. When you have gathered all the information concerning what the child is doing and why he is doing it, you are ready to evaluate the behavior developmentally. This means asking yourself what skills are required for the child to demonstrate that behavior, and what emerging skills are indicated by this behavior. If you were watching a child who had just discovered he can stack blocks one on top of the other, your observation would include the following:

1. Observing the new behavior—seeing the child successfully stacking the blocks.
2. Evaluating the situation—noting that the child is sitting on the floor alone, intently studying the blocks, then picking them up, and putting them in place. You might also note that the child is totally absorbed in this task and that other toys nearby do not attract his attention.
3. Evaluating the developmental implications—asking yourself what skills the child is practicing and what kinds of relationships he is making. You might answer this question as follows:
   Skills being practiced:
   a. Reaching toward and grasping the blocks.
   b. Visually tracking the movement of the hand holding a block.
   c. Moving one block toward another that is already in place.
   d. Placing each block on top of the others so they are aligned in a balanced position.
   Relationships being made:
   a. One object can be placed on top of another.
   b. Objects can be stacked up to make the stack higher.
   c. One block can be put right on the top of the other without them falling over.

The final step in observing involves making a decision concerning the types of activities that will extend the infant's learning experiences. This means you return to the role of facilitator. Returning to the example of the child and the blocks, you might facilitate the child's learning in the following ways:

1. Provide additional blocks for more stacking.
2. Provide different objects for stacking, such as objects differing in color, shape, or size.

3. Engage in stacking activities with the child: you might stack the blocks and have the child knock them over.
4. Challenge the child to relate objects with similar characteristics. You might stack all the skinny blocks here and all the fat ones over there or all the blue ones here and all the red ones over there.

When making decisions relative to the most appropriate ways to extend the learning experiences of a particular child, you should consider the child's personality and temperament, the child's interests, and the ways in which you effectively interact with the child.

There is a considerable amount of trial and error in this approach. Activities you feel sure will appeal to children may not even attract their attention and the things you overlook may be the very ones that do attract their attention. Also an activity that does not succeed at one time may be highly successful a few weeks or months later. The important thing is to attend closely to the messages in the child's behavior and keep trying.

The format for observing. Your observation will be more thorough, objective, and systematic if you follow an outline. Recording your answers on a specific form also gives you a permanent record of those observations. This record enables you to compare the child's movement and behavioral patterns in succeeding developmental phases. These records

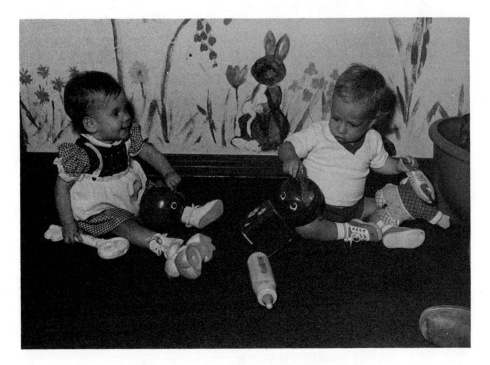

Fig. 3-3. Observing children is a skill. What do you see?

EXAMPLE OF COMPLETED OBSERVATION FORM

NAME OF CHILD: Tommy Saunder   AGE: 20 months

DATE: 4/25/81   TIME: 3:30 PM

ENVIRONMENTAL FACTORS AFFECTING THE CHILD'S PARTICIPATION
Physical surroundings

☐ INDOORS   ☒ OUTDOORS

WEATHER AND TEMPERATURE
Sunny, about 70° F

NATURE AND CONDITION OF PLAYING SURFACE
Level, grassy lawn

LOCATION OF FURNITURE OR OTHER STRUCTURES
Large fenced yard bordered on one side by the house, three large trees along other side, two clothesline poles located in the middle approximately 25 feet apart, three play structures on one end of the yard

AVAILABLE PLAY OBJECTS
A variety of wheeled toys and assorted small toys

OTHER PEOPLE
Approximately 15 children ranging in age from 14 to 24 months; four adult day-care workers

Description of activity
(including movement, social, and emotional behaviors)

Tommy walked over to one of the wagons, took hold of it, and began pulling it around the yard. At first, his path consisted of weaving in and out among objects and other people. Then he began moving in a tight circle. When he had gone around about eight times, another child spotted him and came over to climb into the wagon. Tommy nonverbally welcomed the newcomer and started to pull the wagon. But now it was too heavy. He pulled and pulled, looked puzzled, and then walked around behind the wagon and tried pushing it. That didn't work either. He stood up, put his hands on his hips, and looked around at the other children. A third child joined them. The new child pulled, Tommy pushed, and the rider continued to ride. They began to move in a straight line at an uneven rate because the puller and pusher could not coordinate their actions. Soon they moved too close to one of the clothesline poles and the front end of the wagon ran into it. They continued to push and pull for a little while. Then the child got out of the wagon and all three of them moved toward the pole. They pushed and pulled on it and tried to shake it. Finally they all gave up and walked over to some other toys and soon became absorbed in a new activity.

Continued.

EXAMPLE OF COMPLETED OBSERVATION FORM—cont'd

Developmental implications

SKILLS BEING PRACTICED

    Walking while pulling and pushing an object

    Moving around and between objects

    Pushing and pulling on a stationary object

RELATIONSHIPS BEING MADE

    Recognizing the spatial relationship necessary to move forward, between, and around

    Relating the fact that when another child sat in the wagon, one person could no longer move it

    Relating how the help of another child made it possible to again move the wagon

    Recognizing that the wagon and the pole could not be moved

Decisions concerning how the child's learning can be extended

I could have moved the wagon away from the pole so the children could have continued playing with it, but decided not to since they seemed to be tired of that activity.

At another time, I will encourage Tommy to place some blocks or other light objects in the wagon so he can relate the fact that he can move the wagon with objects in it if the objects are small.

If the opportunity arises, I'll show Tommy how to prevent the wagon (or another toy) from running into a structure, by moving it backward and then sideward.

I may play a follow-the-leader type game with Tommy, challenging him to follow me while he pulls the wagon. We could move between and around objects and structures in a way that will require him to relate the size of the space he must move it through.

---

can also serve to monitor your own ability to observe effectively. By comparing your early experience with later ones, you should be able to note differences in your ability to see, interpret, and extend what the child is learning.

The observation form on these pages contains an outline of the points we have discussed concerning how to effectively observe a child. The example illustrates how the form can be used to record relevant observational information.

SUMMARY

Caregivers must assume four kinds of roles while they are interacting with the child. These are supervisor, participant, facilitator, and observer.

As a supervisor, the caregivers focus on the safety of the children at all times. Efficient supervising involves placing yourself in the room next to high risk areas and signaling to other caregivers the need to intervene.

As participants, caregivers focus on the way they are interacting with the child while participating in a particular activity. To be effective in the role of participant, caregivers must be spontaneous, enthusiastic, relaxed, and above all, they must genuinely enjoy the activity.

As facilitators, caregivers assist the child in developing problem-solving skills. Facilitators assist the child in bridging the gap between things that are known and things that are not known. This is achieved by caregivers providing learning activities that enable the child to make an association between the familiar and the unfamiliar.

As observers, caregivers focus on the child's overt and covert behaviors and interpret what they see and hear. Good observers are selective, objective, and systematic. The process of observing culminates in making decisions concerning activities that will extend the child's learning experiences.

The caregiver's interactions with the infant are the most critical factors affecting the infant's development. Good intentions are not enough. Caregivers must translate their genuine concern into effective actions. This implies that caregivers must be aware of infants' developmental needs and the types of learning activities that will meet these needs. And most importantly, the caregiver must envision that his role includes being a conscientious supervisor, an active participant, an involved facilitator, and a selective observer. A caregiver who effectively functions in these ways is nurturing the child's emotional needs as well as stimulating physical and cognitive development. Fulfilling these roles is challenging and demanding, but the rewards inherent in watching the emergence of the baby's full developmental potential are well worth the effort.

SUGGESTED READINGS

Almy, M.C., and Genishi, C. *Ways of studying children: an observation manual for early childhood teachers.* New York: Teacher's College Press, 1979.

Beaty, J.J. *Observing development of the young child.* Columbus, Ohio: Charles E. Merrill Co., 1986.

Bentzen, W.R. *Seeing young children: a guide to observing and recording behavior.* New York: Delmar Publishers, Inc., 1985.

Boehm, A.E., and Weinberg, P.A. *The classroom observer, a guide for developing observation skills.* New York: Teacher's College Press, 1977.

Cartwright, C.A., and Phillip, G. *Developing observation skills.* New York: McGraw-Hill, Inc., 1974.

Irwin, D.M., and Bushnell, M.M. *Observational strategies for child study.* New York: Holt, Rinehart & Winston, 1980.

Snyder, M., Snyder, R., and Snyder, R., Jr. *The young child as person.* New York: Human Sciences Press, Inc., 1980.

Trotter, R.J. *The play's the thing.* Psychology Today, January, 1987: 27-34.

CHAPTER 4

Relating to young children

The overall relationship between the caregiver and the child is that of friends. This friendship is based on the following attitudes: I am your friend, and I want you to be my friend; I trust you, and I want you to trust me; I respect you, and I want you to respect me; I will help you, and I want you to help me; I will keep you safe, physically and emotionally, which is my primary responsibility. These attitudes can be developed only if you are open and honest. A trusting relationship provides an atmosphere of freedom in which creative play can emerge. Freedom does not mean giving children license to do anything they choose. It means children's play environments are structured by certain rules, and within this structure there are options. These options include the right to be exploratory, inventive, innovative, and creative without fear of failure. These options also include being responsible for one's own safety and respectful of other people. In an atmosphere of this nature, the child's self-respect grows and learning flourishes.

COMMUNICATIONS

The principal source of stimulation during the first months of life is the primary caregiver. A baby learns from watching what this adult does, hearing what this adult says, and feeling how this adult responds. Infants are constantly taking in messages. As soon as they are capable of initiating learned behavioral responses we can observe the effects of this learning. For example, if a caregiver becomes angry when a child does not follow directions, the child learns to react to frustration with anger. Or if a caregiver is always in a hurry and doesn't take the time to let the child put on her own coat, the toddler learns to wait for someone else to do things for her. If a caregiver spends her time trying to amuse the child, rather than giving her the opportunity to play alone, the toddler learns to just stand or sit around until someone comes to play with her. These examples illustrate how the child learns from both our expectations and our actions in everyday situations.

Fig. 4-1. Exploring with "mud play."

Nonverbal communication

An infant is naturally aware of the implied messages in adult actions. A person's body always communicates honestly. Its tone, posture, vitality, tension, proportions and movements all express the person within. The body speaks clearly, revealing the person's character and way of being in the world. It reveals past traumas and present feelings. These signs are a clear language to those who have learned to read it. And young children have this ability, this subtle sensing of energy. It may seem remarkable, or even unbelievable and perhaps frightening, to know that young children are so brilliantly in touch with their senses that they are more aware of you than you are of yourself. But if you compare this ability to that of people's pets, it may seem more plausible. You have probably heard stories about someone's special dog or cat and how this animal seemed to sense its owner's moods, traumas, and special needs. This seems to be the same kind of innate ability belonging to the young child.

Nonverbal Language. There are four ways of communicating without using words. These are (1) facial and bodily expressions, (2) vocal sounds, (3) non-vocal sounds, and (4) touching. It is beyond the scope of this book to discuss all of these factors in detail. We will list some factors in the first three categories and then briefly discuss the subject of touching.

1. *Facial and bodily expressions*
   Facial expressions: interested, natural, forced, blank, open-accepting, rejecting, distorted, happy, sad, surprised, angry, afraid
   Hands and arms: positioning (extending, withdrawing, relaxing, crossing, raising, lowering), gesturing, moving
   Legs and feet: positioning, moving (shifting weight, shuffling)
2. *Vocal sounds:* humming, whistling, smacking, clicking teeth, sucking, coughing, sneezing, laughing, snickering, heavy breathing.
3. *Non-vocal sounds*
   Hands: clapping, tapping fingernails, opening, closing, snapping.
   Feet: stomping, shuffling, wriggling toes, tapping, rubbing together.
4. *Touch:* From the moment of birth, infants are handled and touched by other human beings. This touching becomes an important part of their early communication and interaction with others. As they

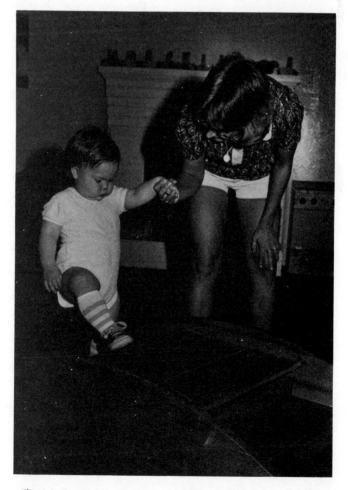

Fig. 4-2. Conveying a negative message by holding onto the child.

are being touched they are discovering things about themselves and their relationships to others. This is why you should take the time to ask yourself, "What am I saying to this child as I touch her?" Possible answers are "I love you," "I don't like what you are doing," "Be careful," "You can't be successful without my help," "Don't move," or "That was good." Sometimes, through our touch, we communicate unintentional or wrong messages. Let's take a balance activity situation as an example. If you grasp the child's arm because you are afraid she will fall, you are conveying a nonverbal message. The message the child receives is, "I know you cannot do the activity and will fall unless I ensure your success." There are ways you can assist in this situation that will convey positive rather than negative messages. One way is to have the child hold your arm. In this way the message to the child is, "I know you can do it, but I'm here if you need me." Another advantage of this approach is that the child is in control of the amount of assistance needed and better able to judge her own success.

Verbal communication

Like our nonverbal expressions, the messages we convey by our words can differ markedly. As you read through this list, you will be able to see how varied word messages can be. We use words to

Ask questions	Describe sensory impressions
Give answers	Verbalize feelings and emotions
Instruct someone	Express hopes and dreams
Give directions	Negate someone's reality
Give commands	Repeat someone else's statements
Threaten	Dramatize real or imaginary events
Report facts	Relate predictions and past events
Tell stories	Express creatively (such as in poetry or songs)
Imitate	

Children's play is influenced by the messages in the words they hear. Some kinds of messages will enhance or extend children's pleasure and learning, whereas other messages will inhibit their active play. You will need to be aware of these different effects as you play with children and as you explore how to use words in the most effective manner.

The meaning in a verbal message is influenced by the type of voice you use and the method of delivery. The following list indicates some of the variations that may affect how children respond.

Pitch	High, low, shrill
Clarity	Smooth, clear, musical, gruff
Intensity	Loud, soft, explosive
Pace	Extremely slow, drawling, fast, very rapid

Attitude   Emotional, non-emotional, loving, friendly, soothing, angry, boastful, superior, authoritarian, abrupt, hesitant, whimpering, whining, tender, casual, intense, secretive

Because so many 1-year-olds and 2-year-olds only talk in single or linked words, adults tend to forget how important it is to talk continuously with them. This is particularly true in group care where young children are frequently asked to follow specific directions. You may find yourself falling into the habit of talking at children rather than talking with them. Talking with children implies an exchange between the two of you. A real conversation requires the interaction of two people. Whenever possible, the conversation should alternate between the caregiver and the child, with the exchange following a pattern such as caregiver-child-caregiver-child.

Avoid talking down to children. Also avoid using negative comments when reprimanding children for misbehaving, when correcting them, or when giving necessary commands or instructions. Being negative is an undesirable form of guidance, not only because it prevents a child from becoming self-directed, but also because it impairs a child's self-concept.

The constructive and productive way of communicating with children is to talk up to them. Talking up to children includes complimenting them on their choice of play materials or on how they are using toys, asking questions about what they are doing, making positive comments about them and their activities, and asking them to make choices only when they clearly have alternatives.

A habit that parents and caregivers fall into is suggesting to children that they have choices when they don't really have them. For example, saying, "Emily, it's time for your nap, okay?" or "Doesn't my little John want to go to the sitter's house?" Questions of this type suggest the child has the option of answering "yes" or "no" when in reality the outcome has already been determined. Growing up believing they have no choices creates a sense of powerlessness in children and is not conducive to development of a healthy self-concept. Ask children to make choices only when they truly have choices. When talking up to young children try to say something that will require the child to respond, either verbally or non-verbally. This engages the child in the conversation thereby reinforcing the communication skill of taking turns. Talking up to children has another advantage as well. When talking up to them, you are training yourself to pay attention to the positive rather than negative aspects of the child's actions.

There are a number of ways to talk up to children while they are playing. You might, for example:

1. Describe what the child has accomplished, such as, "You put the whole puzzle together."

2. Point out something about the child's toys, such as "Melissa, you seem to like the red motorcycle best."
3. Point out how you desire to take part in what the child is doing, such as, "Mike, I'll hold the doll while you dress her."
4. Make a suggestion that will facilitate the child's play, such as, "Kenny, try putting the car at the top of the slide and see what will happen."
5. Respond to the child's question or comment with a statement such as, "Mud pies, yes, I'd love one, thank you."
6. Praise the child by describing his accomplishment, such as, "Ryan, you've been really careful riding the bike today. How does it feel to move in and out of all those obstacles?"

Finally, look at children's faces when you talk with them. This may mean that you have to sit down with them or lift them up so you can talk face-to-face. If you remember that they probably aren't paying attention to you if they are not looking at you, it will prevent misunderstandings and frustrations on your part as well as theirs.

Corresponding messages

Verbal and nonverbal communications may be thought of as two sides of the same coin. Whenever you speak in words, you are also speaking nonverbally and the messages you convey must be similar. That is, your verbal message must be the same as your nonverbal message. We can illustrate how incompatible messages might occur by using the previously mentioned example of the balance activity. Suppose you are grasping the child securely, anticipating that he may fall and at the same time verbally saying, "I know you can do it; you're doing so well." A similar situation would be a toddler coming to you and you saying, "I love you; go play." Sending two simultaneous messages with contradictory meanings is referred to as a double bind. The receiver of these messages becomes confused and disoriented. Relate this to yourself and to relationships with other adults in which you have encountered this double bind phenomenon. Think of how it felt and how it confused your existing realities, then think what this does to children who are learning how to construct reality.

When children are the recipients of contradictory messages, they hear one message, but their intuition tells them something quite different. Let's look then at how the verbal and nonverbal messages we used in the balancing activity example can be changed to corresponding messages. The adult could have said, "I think you might fall, so I will hold your hand." The adult is accurately conveying his concern verbally and is sending the compatible nonverbal message, "I think you will need my help the first time you try." Note that the adult is not sending any messages that contain the element of fear. As mentioned throughout this book, one of the primary learning outcomes essential for young children is to develop the ability to set their own limitations. They will not be able to do this if they are handicapped by adults who transmit their own fears to children. Nor will they be able to discover their own limits if adults continue to assist them. In this example the adult could have the child execute the task alone as soon as possible, but stand near the child in case she chooses to reach out for support.

The second example we used to illustrate conflicting messages involved another aspect of adult-child interaction. The adult verbally expressed affection by saying "I love you" but also verbally rejected the child by saying "go play." This double message has the effect of simultaneously pulling and pushing the child. We are not suggesting that adults interrupt their own pursuits whenever the child has a request. This is neither realistic nor desirable. The child must learn to wait for some things to happen. To achieve this goal and to convey corresponding messages, the adult could have said, "I want to play with you, but I am busy washing the dishes. As soon as I finish, though, I will come and play with you."

Effectively and consistently communicating with children is primarily a matter of being aware and genuine. This type of interaction is summarized in the following five suggestions:

1. Be aware of yourself, your feelings, and your thoughts.
2. Be honest with yourself and with your child about your feelings and thoughts. Do not hide yourself from the child. If the child is constantly whining you could say, "When you whine for what you want instead of asking, I feel frustrated and don't know what to do."
3. Ask yourself continually, "What am I saying to the child? Am I sending corresponding messages or a double bind message?"
4. Realize that you will make mistakes (no one is perfect), but try to be aware of these when they happen.
5. Correct your mistakes as soon as possible by talking with the child about them. Remember, your nonverbal expressions will convey your feelings.

Honestly discussing these feelings and the events surrounding them will establish respect between you and the child.

IMITATION

Young children are naturally imitative and readily learn by imitating adult actions. Using imitation can be an effective method of stimulating learning.

The exact nature of the imitation technique you find to be the most effective will be a reflection of your own personality and the relationship you have with the child. Through our experiences with young children, we have developed a highly effective teaching technique that is a combina-

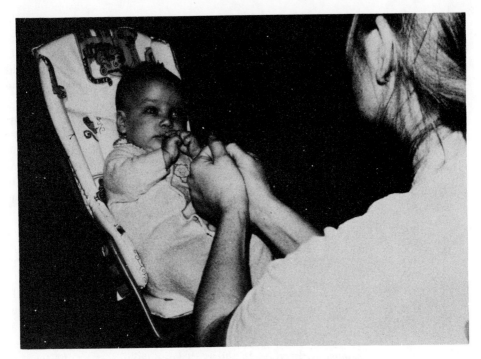

Fig. 4-3. Infants learn by imitating adult actions.

tion of imitation and verbalization. This technique consists of the following five steps:

1. Perform the activity.
2. Verbalize your actions.
3. Reinforce the child's attempts.
4. Stimulate the child verbally.
5. Ask questions.

Performing the activity

The first step in introducing an activity or skill is simply for you to begin doing it. You probably will not need to call the child's attention to what you are doing. Just get involved in the activity yourself, and very shortly the child will become interested and join you. If by chance you do not capture the child's interest, then change activities. Activities that appeal to a child at one time may not interest her at another time. The most important point for you to keep in mind is that you must not give up or force the child to participate. Allow her interest to be self-initiated; then when the child does come to you, you can be sure she is ready to be involved.

Verbalizing your actions

As the child watches you execute the activity, begin verbalizing about what you are doing. For example, you might say, "I am walking backwards. Here I go; I am taking one step backward, two steps backward." The child will usually respond by attempting the activity, and then you can begin verbalizing the child's actions as you both continue to participate. The immediate goal is to enable the child to label the action and to make an association between the word and the action. The ultimate goal is to enable the child to verbalize his own actions.

Reinforcing the child's attempts

Always reinforce the child's attempts. It is not important at this time that the child execute the activity correctly. What is important is that the child keeps on practicing.

Reinforcement means many things to many people. Unfortunately it has been used in many situations to create a dependency syndrome. This happens when parents or caregivers use their relationships as a reinforcer. People may say, "I like the way you are trying to walk backwards," or "I like the way you are watching me." The implied message in these statements is, "what you are doing pleases me." Children eventually may have as their goal to please you, as opposed to discovering themselves. Reinforcing statements that just focus on the child's behavior such as, "You're walking backwards" or "You're moving your feet slowly" avoids the possibility of undermining the child's independence and development of autonomy. Your attention and encouragement will stimulate the child to continue trying, and sooner or later he will acquire the skills necessary to perform the activity. Children at this age are not learning specific skills but are learning how to learn. There will be ample time for them to perfect their skills later when they are more developmentally mature.

If you force a young child and make demands on her, she will learn negative attitudes. We have worked with 3-1/2 year olds who constantly say, "I can't," and refuse to try anything new. This is not a phase these children will outgrow, but a way of thinking and behaving they grew into. The expression, "That's a phase the child will outgrow," is a myth. Phases are manifestations of past experiences, and as a child progresses through the developmental sequence, these manifestations emerge in different forms. They change as the child matures, but they never go away. Therefore, remember to stimulate interest, but do not force the child, and remember to reinforce all attempts with love and warmth. Continuously convey the message that you love the child and that you want the child to keep trying to grow and to be happy.

Verbal stimulation

After you have introduced the skill (first as a model, by doing the activity yourself, then as a participant-model by doing the activity with the child while verbalizing the actions), you can stop participating and just give verbal stimulation. Then you can use the activity as a form of evaluation. Ask yourself these questions: Has the child begun to make the association? Can the child participate in the activity without the visual model, responding only to the verbal cues or stimulations?

After you stop participating, you can verbally assist the child as she executes the activity. If the child is unable to participate alone, simply start over, repeating steps 1 to 3. Begin again by performing the activity, then verbalize your actions, and reinforce the child's attempts. Do this immediately if the child is still attentive or at a later time if she has lost interest. If she appears to have lost interest, never force the child; just keep encouraging her patiently and lovingly.

Asking questions

When the child can successfully complete the first four steps, begin asking questions. The purpose of questioning the child is to heighten awareness and initiate a response. The questions are vital because they assist the child in language acquisition and at the same time reinforce mental associations. The degree of difficulty of the questions, like everything else, depends on the developmental level of the child. The simplest questions only require a yes or a no response. For example, if the child is walking backward you could ask, "Are you walking backward?" If the child is developmentally ready for a more challenging question, there are a variety of ways you can phrase it. You could say, for example, "Are you walking backward or forward?" The first question only requires a yes or a no answer. The second question requires the child to differentiate between backward and forward. It also requires the child to employ the language skill of saying the word "backward." The most difficult questions are open-ended. For example, you may ask the child, "What are you doing?" These questions require the child to select the correct identification of this action from among her entire movement vocabulary. She then could phrase and verbally express the answer.

ASK-SAY-DO

When children have learned how to respond to questioning and are able to do things for themselves, you can use teaching techniques that will develop these skills. We have found that the ask-say-do method works well. This method consists of three sequential steps. First, *ask* the child what activity comes next. If the child can answer the question, the two of you simply move right into the activity that has been named. However, if the child is unable to answer, move to the second step, *say*. In this step, you casually suggest what the next activity will be and offer the child a choice of actions. If the child does not respond to your verbal comments, you will need to move to the third step, *do*. In this step you will model the action so that the child can imitate it. In some instances, you may physically assist the child in performing the action. The following example illustrates how you progress through these three steps.

Step one: Ask. "What could we do now?" Let's assume the child has been playing with some blocks and has lost interest in them. The child might answer your question by saying, "Pick up," or "Clean up," or "Put in box." You could immediately respond in an enthusiastic manner, "That's an excellent idea! You need to put the blocks in the box." At this point, you could assist the child with the cleanup chore, and then the two of you move on to another activity. If the child did not satisfactorily respond to your question, you can employ the second step.

Step two: Say. "When you finish playing with the blocks, you must put them away in the box. You have a choice—do you want to do it by yourself or would you like help?" Then as the child makes a choice, positively reinforce her actions. "I see you have decided you want me to help you." Finally, describe the accomplishment. "Now look, we have picked up all the blocks," or "Jackie and I put the blocks in their house in the box." If the child does not respond to your statement about what must be done, it may be because she doesn't understand, so move to the third step.

Step three: Do. Begin slowly picking up a block while saying, "It is time to clean up. Do you want the little block or the big block to put in the box? How about the little block?" If the child does not respond, you may decide to put your hand on the child's hand and assist her in picking up a block. Remember to be gentle and positive and to talk about what you are doing. This step may not work if the child is tired, or she may simply be too young to understand. In any case, do not force the child, but rather leave this activity for another time.

As you may have noticed, Ask-Say-Do is actually a reversal of the five steps describing imitation techniques. Ask-Say-Do is a more advanced teaching method than imitation techniques because you begin with the assumption that the child will understand you and be willing to respond to your questions. If you find this is not a correct assumption, simply revert to more concrete instructions.

Remember, a child is always learning, so use Ask-Say-Do whenever you are talking with her, whether you are engaged in a daily routine or a play activity.

EVERYDAY TEACHING

There is a very important teaching technique that occurs naturally. This is called incidental teaching because opportunities for its use arise spontaneously. Actually, it is preferable to call it the everyday way of teaching because it is common and occurs every day. The only requirement for everyday teaching is that the child initiate the conversation. In this way you know that the subject of the conversation is important and meaningful to the child. An example of how everyday teaching occurs is illustrated in this typical conversation between a child and a parent.

CHILD: "Gimme another cookie."
PARENT: "What's the magic word?"
CHILD: Looks puzzled.
PARENT: "Can you say, 'Please, give me another cookie?'"

In this example, the parent has used the conversation that the child initiated to teach her how to make a polite request rather than a demand. Many times children will initiate conversations by making requests. These are particularly good times to practice everyday teaching because in these situations children are encouraged by your focused attention to answer your questions. Children are also encouraged if you give them what they have requested.

To use the everyday technique, just follow these steps:

1. Give the child your full attention. When the child speaks to you, look directly at her and listen to what she is saying.
2. Ask a question about what the child has said. Be sure to use an appropriate question rather than one that requires advanced language skills. You want the child to be able to successfully answer you. If you cannot think of a good question immediately, let the opportunity pass rather than making the child wait.
3. Give a hint or tell the child the answer. If the child doesn't answer you right away, give a hint or describe what you want her to say so she can imitate you. Do not keep the child waiting for what she requested or prolong the conversation by trying to make the child answer you.
4. Repeat the child's description or the answer to the questions to reinforce the language skills. Give the child what she asked for even if she does not answer. Do not withhold the item until she speaks for you, or you are no longer teaching the child, but manipulating her. Teaching results in later self-initiations while manipulations result in later expressions of anger and oppositional behaviors.

SAFETY TRAINING

Children are born with built-in protective mechanisms that ensure survival. Even the newborn instinctively protects herself. A strong blink reflex protects her eyes from excess light. If one part of her body is exposed to a markedly lower temperature, the whole body changes color and temperature, she pulls in her limbs to reduce the exposed body surface, and finally begins to cry and shiver to improve circulation. If an object is placed over an infant's mouth and nose, she will actively resist its smothering effect. She will mouth the object and then twist her head violently from side to side in an attempt to remove it. If these maneuvers fail, she will cross each arm over her face to try to dislodge the object. These examples illustrate the fact that the newborn is basically a safety-oriented being.

Through natural exploratory activities, the infant's safety sense is gradually refined. This learning process is guided by adult interaction rather than by control. This interaction assists children in becoming aware of their own limitations instead of being forced to adhere to the false limitations imposed by adults. False limitations cause the child to become dependent on adult control for safety and survival. The real danger exists in the fact that children are unaware of this dependency state and, as a result, set false limits on their previous activities. This creates situations in which accidents are destined to occur. When adults assume complete lifelong responsibility for a child's safety, 24 hours a day, one-on-one supervision is required. This is an undesirable and unrealistic goal for any adult. And it explains why in emergency rooms one often hears comments such as, "I just took my eyes off him for a second and..." or "The phone rang and the next thing I knew..."

The question then is twofold: how do children gradually become aware of their own limitations, and how can you assist rather than inhibit this process? First, you must be aware that children set their own limitations based on their successes and failures. Therefore you must allow children to fail. This fact can be exemplified by watching a 2-year-old exploring her ability to jump down from various objects.

The child naturally begins by jumping from very low objects. Then, when she has developed a sense of mastery by having been repeatedly successful, she will create a new challenge by moving up to a higher object. This progression continues until the child is faced with a situation in which she cannot succeed. When she recognized her inability to successfully meet the demands of this challenge, she set her own limitation. She has also learned by doing rather than by being told what to do.

Learning theory tells us that if people fail repeatedly they will stop trying. In the foregoing example, we do not want the child to stop jumping. We must interact with the child in a manner that will enable her to view her failure as a positive and necessary learning experience. The concept we want her to learn is that, "You have not failed; you just haven't learned how." To attain this learning outcome, you would first go to the child, and after being sure there are no injuries, you would reinforce her for trying. You can then use the situation as a learning medium through a variety of approaches. The approach you use to attain your goal must be determined by the cues you pick up from the child. She may be angry and the intensity of her anger is an important factor. Just think how difficult it is for you to learn when you are extremely upset! First you must let the child release the anger by allowing her to just be angry. After the emotion has been expressed, direct her to another activity in which she can experience success. Another possibility is that the child may be experiencing fear rather than anger. In this case, first check for injuries, then warmly reassure her (probably by holding and cuddling). When her self-confidence and enthusiasm have returned, direct her to a new success-oriented activity. If the child does not seem to be emotionally reacting to her failure, you can simply point out the "not yet" message and move on to another activity. A "not yet" message communicates the idea that "you haven't learned how to do this yet." We prefer to use these kinds of messages rather than implying that the child has failed. This distinction is an important one because "not yet" messages stimulate participation whereas failure messages discourage the child.

Possible ways to vary activities are limitless, and if you remain alert to learning opportunities, you will discover a variety of approaches. Continuing with the example above, you might want to redirect the play to focus on the concepts of high and low, and develop into a high-low game. The child could jump from a low box, and then you could jump from the same box. Next, you could jump from a higher box and challenge the child to imitate your actions. You could point out that the highest box is very high so you won't try jumping from it right now. Instead you will practice on the other boxes, and another time you can both try jumping from the highest box. Interactions of this nature are possible in situations that occur throughout the day, and similar procedures should be followed whenever possible.

There are actually three aspects of this safety training. First, you must constantly encourage children to set safety limits. Second, you must help children to recognize that these limits constantly change. Finally, and perhaps most importantly, you must assist children in becoming aware that the limitations are under their control. This learning process is the result of mutual trust. The adult trusts the child to establish reasonable limits, and the child trusts the adult for assistance as these limits continue to change.

Assisting the child in safety training does not decrease your responsibilities concerning supervision. Both supervision and safety training are responsibilities of a primary caregiver. During your initial contacts with the child you will need to assess her ability to set safety limits. Your observations concerning this ability can then serve as the starting point in the child's ongoing safety training.

SUMMARY

Ideally, the relationship between the primary caregiver and the infant is that of friends, and the relationship is based on mutual trust. In this kind of atmosphere, the child enjoys freedom while learning to be responsible.

The caregiver is constantly communicating with the infant and the messages are often nonverbal. Infants are keenly aware of the implied messages in adult actions. Nonverbal messages are conveyed through facial and bodily expressions, through vocal and nonvocal sounds, and through touching. The messages conveyed by words can differ markedly from nonverbal messages. We not only use words in many different contexts, but also influence their meaning by the type of voice we use and the method of delivery. It is vital that adults convey similar verbal and nonverbal messages because contradictory messages leave the child confused and disoriented.

Children are great imitators; therefore imitation can be an effective way of stimulating learning. The teaching techniques that have proved most effective include both imitation and verbalization.

Everything children do is a potential learning experience. Utilize these teachable moments by encouraging children to talk about what they are doing. This enables children to pay close attention to their actions as well as to enhance their verbal learning.

One of the most important areas of caregiver responsibility is the safety training of children. Safety training is an ongoing process that consists of (1) constantly encouraging children to set safety limits, (2) helping children to recognize that these limits constantly change, and (3) assisting children to become aware that the limits are under their control. It must be remembered, however, that safety training supplements rather than replaces adequate supervision.

SUGGESTED READINGS

Berends, P.B. *Whole child/whole parent*. New York: Harper & Row Publishers Inc. 1983.

Cataldo, C.Z. *Infant & toddler programs: a guide to very early childhood education*. Menlo Park, California: Addison-Wesley Publishing Company, 1983.

Guillaume, P. *Imitation in children*. Chicago: University of Chicago Press, 1968.

Kurtz, R. and Prestera, H. *The body reveals*. New York: Harper & Row Publishers Inc. 1977.

Montague, A. *Touching*. New York: Perennial, 1971.

Snyder, M., Snyder, R., and Snyder, R., Jr. *The young child as person*. New York: Human Sciences Press, Inc., 1980.

Yando, R., Seitz, V., and Zigler, E. *Imitation: a developmental perspective*. New York: John Wiley & Sons, Inc., 1978.

CHAPTER 5

Constructing reality

At birth infants are totally unaware of themselves and the world that surrounds them. They are not yet capable of noticing and relating what is going on in the world. Because infants often appear so passive, many adults fail to recognize the importance of this period of development. Adjusting to the world outside the womb and undergoing the rapid developmental changes characteristic of the first few months of life require all of the infant's energy. And even though they are not actively responding to much of the external stimulation provided by caregivers, they are taking in parts of it. As infants' sense modalities and nervous systems become more mature, they take in more messages and begin to respond. And this early sensory stimulation is the new material from which infants begin to construct the reality of themselves and the world.

DEVELOPMENT OF THE INFANT'S REALITY

Erik Erikson, the famous personality theorist, states that the primary psychosocial task of the first year of life is development of a sense of trust versus a sense of mistrust. Therefore attentive care and gentle handling of infants results in them becoming trusting children. Neglect or harshness has the opposite effect, causing children to become fearful, anxious, and insecure. People used to think that if you loved a child too much, you would spoil him. We now know that a person cannot be loved too much, especially in the first year of life. These first feelings of closeness and *unconditional* acceptance become the infant's first and most enduring experience. The reality of this trusting relationship becomes the perpetuating force behind the development of all other relationships. The infant who has a positive sense of himself will also have self-assurance. This basic belief in himself will enable the infant to take the risks necessary in exploratory learning. And in time he will be capable of being a self-reliant learner.

Constructing a reality is a gradual process. We can think of it as being like a mosaic. Bit by bit, the infant enlarges a picture of his universe by fitting each new piece into the whole. Thus his reality gradually becomes larger and more complex. But the child's picture of his reality always centers around himself. This is the self he sees reflected in the caregiver's actions.

There are several aspects of the child's reality. We will discuss the five aspects the child develops by being a dynamic self. These are the reality of "me," object reality, spatial reality, causal reality, and temporal reality.*

The reality of "me"

How the child constructs the reality of himself has been discussed extensively in previous chapters. However, mention of an important aspect of this self has yet to be introduced. This is the child's awareness of the physical "me." Body awareness is an essential aspect of the child's reality. Throughout a child's entire lifetime, he will perceive all other physical realities in reference to his own body.

Body awareness is both cognitive (mental) and affective (feeling). Children must cognitively come to know all of their body parts (body part identification): their location, their function, and how they relate to the rest of the body. The affective aspect of body awareness includes the feelings you have about your body and your ability to sense and experience your body. Many of these feelings originate early in children's lives from the way they are touched, held, and cared for. Children who are gently touched and fondled will associate pleasure-giving sensations with their bodies, whereas children who are handled in a rough manner will not have an experiential basis for developing these positive associations. Children's feelings about their bodies often reflect their parents' attitudes toward physical and biological functions. If parents have open, positive attitudes about such things as eating, elimination, and sex, the child will reflect these attitudes. However, if the child is forced to eat and to eliminate, and if elimination and sex are something "dirty," or something "one doesn't talk about," these attitudes will be transferred to the child. Because the child's early learning has such an impact on all later learning, it is essential to have the kind of experiences that will facilitate development of positive attitudes about the body.

Object reality

A young infant translates visual sensations into images that form mental pictures. These pictures are only present in the baby's mind while the actual object is being viewed. When the object is removed from the baby's visual field, the mental picture of it also disappears. The young infant's reality is limited to things that are in the here and now. For the baby, out of sight is out of mind. But then as the baby continues to experience and to mature, she becomes capable of comprehending the fact that an object's existence is not dependent on it being physically present. The infant's realization that objects still exist even though she is not looking at them or acting on them

---

*For additional information concerning the origin of these concepts, see the references to Piaget cited in the suggested readings at the end of this chapter.

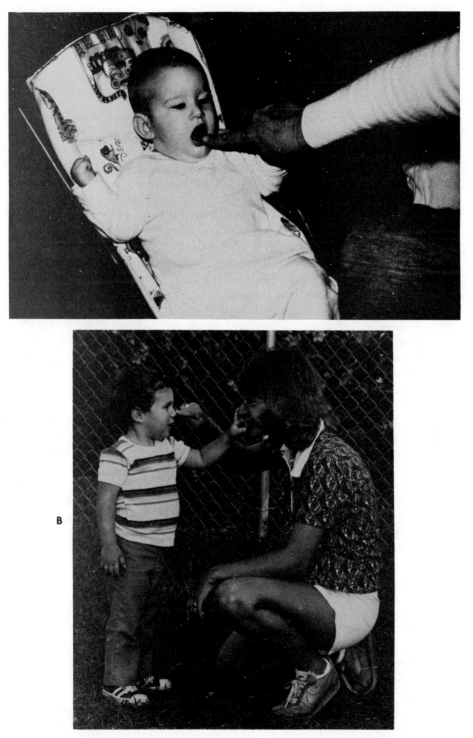

Fig. 5-1. A, Body awareness begins with the vague recognition of "me" versus "not me." **B**, Body awareness skills progress from recognition of one's own body parts to recognition of the body parts of other people.

is called *object permanence*. One of the most important aspects of object permanence is the infant's recognition that the body is also an object and that it exists among other objects.

Spatial reality

The development of spatial reality is dependent on the development of object reality. The infant must first be able to distinguish the reality of objects because the concept of space is understood only as a function of objects. Very young infants perceive space as a collection of unrelated spaces. Gradually they begin to view space as a single unitary whole in which everything is located.

The development of the young child's ability to perceive her own body as being separate from other objects is the beginning of spatial reality. From this point on, the child's body will serve as the central reference point as she interacts with the physical reality of the world; that is, she will perceive the locations and dimensions of all other objects in space in relation to her own body. Reaching and grasping evidence the beginning of the infant's spatial reality. She begins to reach out for something located in space. Gradually she begins to detect that things may be located in different directions and on different levels and that the sizes and shapes of people and things may differ. This early learning becomes the functional foundation of the individual's ability to relate to the physical world.

Causal reality

The term *causal reality* refers to the ability to make cause-and-effect relationships. This ability develops by the infant having a wide variety of experiences that enable him to form associations and make relationships. Gradually he begins to understand that certain actions bring about certain results. For example, when the baby cries the caregiver appears. So the baby forms an association: crying (the cause) makes the caregiver appear (the effect). Eventually the infant will make the kinds of relationships that enable him to foresee an effect given the cause and to infer a cause given only its effect.

Temporal reality

The development of temporal (time) reality is extremely difficult to document because time is an abstract concept. It appears that temporal reality first emerges as a vague sense of duration involving the concepts of *before* and *after*. Then as the child's capacity to remember increases, she becomes capable of envisioning that events occur one after another. This enables her to reconstruct short sequences of events. The development of temporal reality is marked by the child's awareness of time as a generalized medium like space, in which self and objects can be located relative to each other. This is why comparisons and contrasts must be used whenever possible.

THE EFFECT OF LANGUAGE

When children develop the ability to translate sensory input and mental pictures into words, their reality undergoes marked change. Mastering language enables children to manipulate words in their minds and to manipulate actual objects with their bodies. It also enables children to substitute words for actions as a form of communication.

Language skills like all other skills must be learned. Movement activities are the natural learning medium for language skills for two reasons. One reason is that language development parallels motor development. Thus as the child's basic movement patterns are emerging, so is the capacity to associate words and actions. Another reason is that movement activities provide the child with concrete (real) examples of things that words name and describe. This places the word in a real context, which the child can experience again and again.

Chapter 6 is devoted entirely to activities that utilize movement as a medium for learning both physical and conceptual skills. The actitivies are presented in developmental sequence to emphasize the parallels between the development of physical skills and language skills. The natural relationships between different types of learning are highlighted. This enables parents and caregivers to participate in the child's learning processes in a way that maximizes the meaning of the activity as well as the child's physical development.

The phases of constructing reality

We have divided infancy (birth to 2 years) into five developmental phases. These divisions are used only to clarify our discussion of the sequential changes that occur as infants construct functional pictures of themselves and of the world. Both the divisions and the age designations are arbitrary. We divided the phases according to distinct changes in the infant's ability to function. The designated ages simply approximate when these changes often occur. The divisions and ages are not meant to be used as standards for developmental change. Rather their intended purpose is to focus the reader's attention on the sequential nature of change and how these changes affect the infant's developmental needs. The five developmental phases we have designated are (1) the adjustment phase (birth to 1 month), (2) the sensory phase (1 to 4 months), (3) the object phase (4 to 8 months), (4) the space phase (8 to 12 months), and (5) the persistence phase (12 to 24 months). These phases parallel the five stages of the sensorimotor period as described by Piaget (Flavell, 1963).

THE ADJUSTMENT PHASE

Imagine yourself lying serenely, curled up in a warm, safe environment where sensory stimulation is minimal and where no one bothers you. Then suddenly you are turned upside down, thrust into an opening that isn't quite

Fig. 5-2. The phases of constructing reality.

big enough, yanked through it anyway, spanked on the butt, scrubbed clean, dressed, and placed in the midst of sensory bombardment. Welcome to the world; you are now a newborn! Seems a bit drastic, doesn't it? But somehow we all survived.

Newborns are not as helpless as they appear. They are immediately capable of executing the activities necessary to sustain life. Newborns can breathe, suck, swallow, and eliminate waste material. They can look, hear, taste, smell, feel, turn their heads, and signal for help. However, newborns do have many limitations. Their entire existence centers around their bodily needs. They sleep 14 to 18 hours a day and, on the average, are alert and comfortable for only about 30 minutes in a 4-hour period. The reflexes that govern their movements are automatic and beyond their control. Yet, from the very beginning, the infants can experience various sensations. They can feel changes in temperature, detect differences in tastes, smells, and sounds; and they see! They will try to focus on a brightly colored object 8 to 12 inches in front of their eyes, and within 3 weeks they are able to distinguish a human face. Babies are also very sensitive to touch and to pressure. Your first means of communicating your feelings to your baby is through touch. Skin contact and warmth, especially from the parent's body, are probably the most potent sources of stimulation in the first few months of life. Babies are like radar screens, picking up vibrations from your handling. They can sense gentle fondling as well as roughness or uncertainty. Touch is the most important factor in establishing the infant's first intimate relationship, and this is why you need to be aware of the quantity and quality of your physical contacts with the baby.

The infant's adjustment to the world does not require any special activities, only those normally associated with loving, attentive care. Therefore the caregiver's interaction with the newborn should communicate genuine affection. This includes the tone of your voice and your facial expressions as well as touching, tender stroking, and consistent handling. It is possible to overstimulate an infant, and for this reason you should be attentive to signs of fatigue.

Stroking the infant elicits reflexive responses, and thereby provides necessary daily physical activity. Therefore you should stroke different parts of

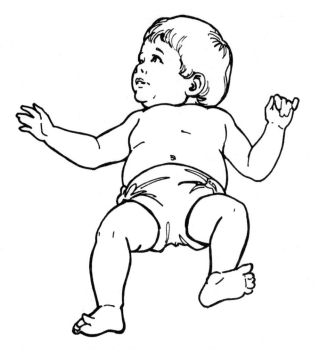

Fig. 5-3. The tonic neck reflex.

the infant's body. Some of the body parts you should stroke and the actions this will stimulate are as follows:

1. The cheek or mouth—the head turns, the tongue moves toward the stroking source, and the mouth begins to suck.
2. The palms of the hands and the soles of the feet—the hands and feet make grasping motions.
3. The outside soles of the feet—the toes extend outward fanlike, with the big toe pointing upward.
4. The top sides of the hands and feet—the hand or foot withdraws, arches, and then returns to a grasp.
5. The legs and upper region of the trunk—the opposite leg or hand crosses over to push your hand away.

Placing the infant in different positions also stimulates reflexive actions. Some of these are as follows:

1. Hold the infant up as though she were standing, and press the feet to a surface—the infant will make walking motions.
2. Lay the infant's front body surface in shallow water, supporting her body by holding onto the chest—the infant will display swimming motions.
3. Lay the infant down on a flat surface—the infant will turn her head to the side and lift her chest by pushing with her arms.

4. Place the infant on her back and turn her head to one side—the infant will assume what is called *the fencer's position*, that is, the body arches away from the side the baby is facing. The arm extends on the side the infant is facing, whereas the arm and leg flex on the opposite side (this is called the tonic neck reflex).

These examples illustrate that gentle handling and various ways of holding and positioning the baby stimulate the kinds of movement activities that meet the infant's developmental needs during the first few weeks of life.

THE SENSORY EXPERIENCES PHASE

We have designated the developmental phase of approximately 1 to 4 months of age as the sensory experiences phase. By calling it the period of sensory experiences, we are emphasizing that it is in this span of time that the infant's sensory modes rapidly develop. These early months are also a critical time in the initial development of intersensory associations. At first, infants' perceptions are merely a collection of sensations. They are not yet able to distinguish between self and objects or self and space. Infants' inherent, reflexive actions serve as their first learning medium. For example, the sucking reflex initiates the actions of the mouth, and the mouth in turn becomes one of the infant's primary sources of exploration. Gradually the infant becomes capable of associating sensations from the mouth with sensations from other sense modalities. The stages of development in which sucking and vision become coordinated can be readily observed. For a period of time after birth, infants suck with their eyes closed. Gradually they begin to suck with their eyes open. Now whenever something in their visual field attracts their attention, they will stop sucking. They must either suck or watch. They cannot do both at the same time because they cannot process information coming in from more than one sense modality.

Hand watching is another example of how reflexes function as a learning medium for the infant. Hand watching begins with the tonic neck reflex. This reflex causes the baby's arm to raise automatically on the same side as his head is turned. This brings the hand into direct view of the eyes and becomes the first step in the development of hand-eye coordination. A similar example is the infant's hand-to-mouth association. Placing the hand in the mouth is a satisfying sensory experience that initiates further action. You can observe this progression by placing a toy in the infant's hand. Soon he directs it to his mouth and begins sucking on it. By doing this, he is beginning to associate the sensory experiences of touching and tasting. The visual aspect is soon added with hand watching. This action begins with the infant holding his hands in front of himself. He watches as his fingers move slowly, looks back and forth between his hands, brings his hands together, and grins as they clutch each other. The infant is beginning to associate the fact that his hands and feet are extensions of his body, and this marks the beginning of his ability to distinguish between "me" and "not me."

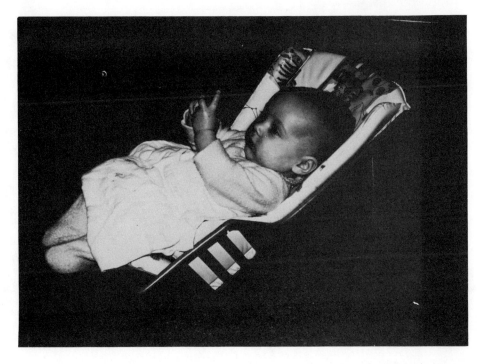

Fig. 5-4. Handwatching permits the infant to begin distinguishing between "me" and "not me."

Near the end of the sensory experiences phase, the grasp reflex recedes, enabling the infant to move freely, to touch, and to voluntarily grasp with the fingers. All these actions prepare the infant to progress to the next phase of development in which he will be handling objects.

Enriching sensory experiences

At first most of your interaction with a young infant will consist of touching, holding, snuggling, and rocking her. During this physical contact you may speak softly, coo, or sing to the baby. When the infant receives this kind of genuine affection, she usually will respond by relaxing and either looking into your face intently or closing her eyes. These are very important sensory experiences. The infant's relaxation manifests positive adjustment to you and to the world, and her visual response provides essential sensory input. And although the infant does not respond to auditory stimulation, she does hear you and is processing the sensory input in some way.

These early forms of positive stimulation are extremely important. The more attractive and pleasant sensations the infant receives, the more she will want to see, hear, and feel. Her vocabulary of sensory experiences will also become greater. If you gently invite her to respond, she is free to accept or reject the sensory input. This is a vital factor because only the infant can

Fig. 5-5. Infants need genuine affection consisting of as much touching and physical contact as possible.

know her energy and interest levels. This is why you should let the infant regulate her participation and never force her attention or response.

The following activities exemplify ways you can stimulate sensory experiences in the young infant. You should view these activities as ways to begin sensory stimulation and as ideas to spark your creativity and ingenuity. We anticipate that you will find many other ways of utilizing sources of stimulation as you explore with the infant.

Activities to enhance sensory experiences
Family Faces

PURPOSES: To provide interesting visual stimulation that will enable the baby to (1) practice using eye muscles to focus on a stable, two-dimensional visual field, (2) learn to associate a picture with a person, and (3) derive pleasure from seeing a pictorial representation of the human beings who love and care for him.

MATERIALS: A large photograph or enlarged snapshot of the baby's family. The faces of the family members should portray feelings of happiness, pleasure, comfort, and warmth.

Tape the picture on the ceiling above your baby's head, so that when he is lying on his back, in bed, he can look up and see it.

ACTIVITY: When the baby is lying awake in his bed, occasionally point out who is in the picture. Also, point out and identify yourself. Be enthusiastic and use definite gestures to attract and hold the baby's attention.

VARIATIONS:

1. Replace the family picture with a picture of the baby, a favorite toy, or an attractive design. Be sure the baby likes the picture and is attracted to it.

2. Wear a T-shirt on which a large picture has been transferred. Stand where the baby can focus on the picture. When he can focus on the picture with you standing still, begin swaying from side to side or stepping backward one or two steps.

    a. Move to the side slightly so the baby will have to turn his head to see you. Gradually move farther around him until you are beside, then behind him.

    b. Hold the baby on your lap in a position that will permit him to focus on the picture on your T-shirt. Sway from side-to-side and back-and-forth.

Fish Freaks

PURPOSES: (1) To stimulate the use of eye muscles in tracking moving objects, (2) to encourage reaching out toward moving objects, and (3) to provide a visual stimulus that is constantly changing to nourish the sensory input necessary in conceptual development.

MATERIALS: A fish tank placed adjacent to the crib or a plastic pouch that attaches to the side of the crib, and a variety of brightly colored fish.

ACTIVITY: Introduce the baby to the fish by pointing them out and enthusiastically talking about them. Periodically draw the baby's attention to the fish.

Hand Watching

PURPOSE: To provide a visually attractive stimulus that will encourage visual tracking and the development of hand-eye coordination.

MATERIALS: Mittens that fit the child's hands. Cut the finger and thumb parts of the mittens off, so that the infant's fingers and thumb are free to be sucked. Gloves may also be used or colored cloth wrapped around the palm of the hand. Red mittens, gloves, or cloth are excellent.

ACTIVITY: Place the mittens on the infant's hands and allow time for her to explore. If the child appears uncomfortable or resists having the mittens on, remove them. If she is attracted by them, let her reach, rub, and grasp while wearing them; then remove them. Place the mittens within the baby's visual field so she can explore them as objects separate from her body. Repeat the activity another day if the baby seems to enjoy it.

Mobiles

PURPOSES: To provide a changing assortment of objects that will stimulate the baby to (1) use the eye muscles to focus on a visual arrangment, (2) practice reaching and grasping, and (3) detect characteristics of objects.

MATERIALS: Assorted objects, such as empty cans and small boxes, metal and wooden spoons, interesting looking hats, scarves, men's ties, ribbons, a glove or a mitten, different colored pieces of foil made into shapes, a mirror, stuffed toys, pie tins, rattles, or wind chimes.

ACTIVITY: Suspend several of the objects from a piece of elastic string across the baby's bed. Change the objects at frequent intervals to maintain interest. Select objects that match the baby's developmental level. For example, use objects with high visual appeal for the very young infant who is not yet reaching or grasping (such as a variety of shapes made from different colors of foil). Then, when the baby begins to reach for the things, substitute objects he can easily grasp such as the glove, stuffed toy, rattle, or scarf.

VARIATIONS:

1. Use clothespins to attach objects to a clothes hanger and suspend them from the ceiling above the baby's crib.
2. Observe the baby and determine which objects attract and hold his attention. Then, as times goes on, substitute new objects that resemble these.
3. Vary the location of the objects so the baby must look or reach in a slightly different direction. Place some of these where the baby can touch and kick them with his foot.
4. Assist the baby in noticing new objects by shaking and moving them within the baby's visual field. If he is in the reach and grasp stage, have him touch, rub, and grasp the object. Then hang up the objects and make them move.

Note: You should always talk to the baby about the objects, their location, and their action because this provides essential verbal stimulation.

Where Did It Go

PURPOSE: To practice movements involving hand-eye coordination.

MATERIALS: One of the baby's favorite toys or an object that attracts her attention.

ACTIVITY: Hold the object at the infant's eye level so she can focus on it. When she has focused, move the object very slowly, trying to encourage the baby to follow the object with her eyes. Move the object in front of the child. Notice when the child loses sight of the object and whether she is capable of moving her head or torso to follow the object. If the child is capable of extending her visual field by moving, encourage more practice of this movement by changing the path of the object. You may want to move the object up and down as the child follows it with her

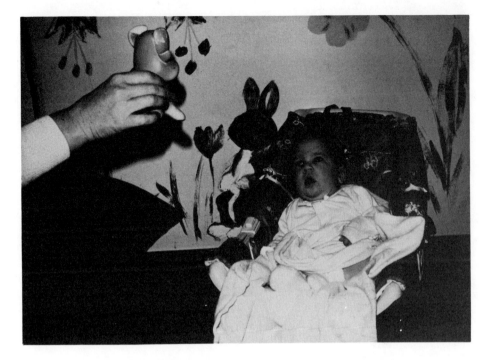

Fig. 5-6. Visual tracking is an essential developmental skill.

eyes, or create pathways in space using waving motions to give the child further practice. If the child is not able to extend her visual field by head or torso movements, continue moving various objects from side to side directly in front of the child.

Sight-seeing

PURPOSES: (1) To give the baby an opportunity to observe a variety of objects and environmental factors and (2) to provide a "change of scene" from that experienced by the infant in his crib.

MATERIALS: The home and neighborhood environment.

ACTIVITY: Carry the baby around the house or a building pointing out interesting objects and the way they move. Point out things such as the actions of a pet, steam rising from boiling water, or the vibrations of a washing machine. Look out the window and point out the trees swaying, the rain dropping or running down the windows, the leaves falling, or the movements of animals, people, or vehicles.

VARIATIONS:

1. Take the baby outside and walk around, pointing out objects and actions.
2. Take the baby to a place such as the grocery store and point out interesting events and different environmental factors.

My Name

PURPOSE: To enable the baby to begin recognizing her name and developing a sense of self.

MATERIALS: None.

ACTIVITY: Have someone else hold the baby while you position yourself in front of her within her visual field. Say her name over and over until she responds by looking at you as you say it.

VARIATIONS:

1. Sing the baby's name.
2. Move closer and whisper her name.

Body Massage

PURPOSE: To stimulate the sensation of being warmly touched and rubbed.

MATERIALS: Baby oil, lotion, or powder.

ACTIVITY: Gently massage the baby's entire body while talking to him in a way that explains what you are doing. For example, you could say, "I'm rubbing your arms," "I'm rubbing your legs," or "I'm rubbing your feet."

Body Stretching

PURPOSE: To stimulate the sensation of the muscles and the joints being gently stretched.

Fig. 5-7. Body-stretching activities provide an ideal medium for adult-child interaction.

MATERIALS: None

ACTIVITY: Calmly, but warmly, and enthusiastically explain to the baby what you are doing as you move her body in the following ways:

1. With the baby on her back, let her hold your thumbs, then extend her arms completely out to the side, down to her side, up over her head, and across her chest.

2. With the baby on her back, support both legs under the knee joint, and toss her legs gently up and down.

3. Holding onto both legs, raise them to touch her face, then spread them to the side.

4. Alternating legs, push the knee to the chest in a walking fashion.

Note: Be careful that your movements are slow, gentle, and easy, and if the baby is not enjoying the activity, *don't do it!*

THE OBJECT EXPERIENCES PHASE

The quiet of the first 4 months dramatically comes to an end, and the infant seems to burst forth to explore the world. The period between 4 to 8 months is characterized by the infant beginning to "reach out" into the environment. Infants no longer are content just to be sensory and to watch and listen to people and things. They now demand to be sensorimotor. Their

Fig. 5-8. Just as infants reach out to their environment for objects, they also reach out for physical affection.

eyes, fingers, mouths, and entire bodies become more and more active. They begin to indicate that objects should be located close enough so that they can reach, grasp, shake, hold, turn, feel, and taste them. This is the reason we have designated this developmental period as the object experiences phase.

The infant's ability to see, handle, turn, suck, and reach increases his awareness of the stability and permanency of objects. Prior to this time, the infant perceived objects as a series of things that mysteriously appeared and disappeared from her visual field. Now she is capable of visually following a moving object and of anticipating where an object will move. You can test this ability by holding an object in front of the infant long enough for him to visually focus on it. Then drop the object and watch the infant's reaction. An infant who, in an earlier developmental state, would have simply stared at the spot where you released the object, will now lean over to look for it on the floor.

The simple activity of an infant handling an object may appear purposeless to an adult, but a great deal of learning is actually occurring. For example, an infant attempting to construct the reality that the shape of an object remains the same although its visual appearance may change will turn the object all around and move it toward herself. You can experience some of what the infant is actually perceiving if you pick up a block or another one of your child's toys. Examine it closely, paying attention to how the shape seems to change as you turn the object around or place it on the table in various positions. This is what the infant is trying to comprehend as she studies the objects in her world.

The infant will now also try to recapture a lost object. This is a further indication of her developing ability to perceive the permanency of objects. She will now search outside her field of vision for an object that drops out of sight. However, she usually gives up immediately if the vanished object does not soon appear. It is fascinating to watch an infant who has had an object slip out of her hand. You can determine her developmental level by observing whether or not she looks for the object, how long she searches, and if she moves her head or body to continue the search.

There are several signs of an infant's growth toward object permanency. An infant who has been playing with a block will leave it for a while, and then relocate it without error or hesitation when he wants to resume play. The infant can also anticipate a whole object by seeing only a part. For example, if you take a stuffed toy and cover it completely with a blanket, the infant will not search for it. However, if you leave a part showing (such as the head or tail), the infant will find the toy. Although the child is now rapidly advancing toward the development of object permanency, he still seems to believe that objects can alternate between being real and unreal. The ability to conceptualize the reality of objects that are not physically present will emerge in a later phase of development.

As infants are developing prehension (the ability to reach and grasp), their actions are becoming purposeful and intentional. No longer must they passively wait until the caregiver offers stimulation. Now when they want something, they reach out for it and grasp to gain control of it. At this point, babies are able to establish cause-and-effect relationships. You can use a mechanical toy to assess an infant's ability to make these relationships. Obtain a windup toy such as a bear that plays a drum. Sit in front of the child, close enough so that he can reach out and touch your hands. Wind up the toy and watch the child anticipate the action. When the toy runs down or stops, observe the child's reaction and the way he communicates with you. If the toy held the child's interest, he will want you to repeat the action. Note how your child communicates this to you. Infants in the 4 to 8 month age range will typically respond with some type of vigorous movement such as waving their arms, kicking their feet, or striking their hands against the floor. Older children who are more aware of cause-and-effect relationships will behave differently. For example, a typical response of infants 8 to 12 months of age will be to touch your hand, indicating that your hand caused the action and they want you to do it again because it was fun. A typical

Fig. 5-9. Prehension is the ability to visually locate and reach out and grasp an object.

response of children 12 to 18 months of age will be to pick up the toy and hand it to you, making the association between your hand and the action of the toy. Older children usually make an effort to be their own agents of cause and effect by winding up the toy themselves.

During this phase, infants' object experiences are facilitated by the development of their movement abilities. Some infants will roll over, sit up, and crawl. Others will lie on their backs, looking and listening, then respond by reaching and grasping. In other words, there is no specific time schedule for the emergence of these abilities. The important thing is that you are aware of when the infant is developmentally ready and that you provide the type of stimulation needed for a particular movement pattern to develop.

The infant lying in his bed wiggling, squirming, and reaching soon discovers he can arch his back and look upside down at things, twist in all directions, roll, flop, and then crawl. In preparation for crawling, an infant will devise a personalized "worming" skill to get across the room. Sometimes this evolves from twisting and rolling movements.

Frequently when flopping or crawling, a baby first moves in a backward direction. He may be attempting to move forward, but his lack of sense of direction causes confusion, which may be quite frustrating to him. The ability to move forward will soon emerge if the baby continues to practice. Therefore, in your role you must provide lots of love, positive reinforcement, and encouragement.

During this phase some infants will begin making an effort to stand. Adults need to be aware, however, that the infant's attempts to stand do not mean she is saying, "I am ready to walk." It just means she is saying, "I am ready to stand." You must be patient. Standing is a skill that requires a great deal of body control. This control develops as a result of extensive practice, just like any other skill.

Many infants learn to stand easily. However, getting back down to the floor may be quite a different matter. Infants may spend several frustrating weeks learning how to sit back down. They will fall and try again; fall and try again. If your infant continues to experience difficulty getting down from her new standing position, try to teach her how—*but don't do it for her.* Stand her up at your knees, bend her slightly at the middle, and then gently push her downward so that she half falls into a sitting position. Repeat this over and over, then wait a few days and see what happens. Whatever you do, don't overprotect the infant and don't transfer your fears to her. What she is undergoing is perfectly normal, and there is no reason she should sustain any injuries if allowed to progress at her own rate.

In addition to the whole body movements that are developing at this time, reaching and grasping skills are also progressing. The baby's thumb now functions in opposition to the fingers, making it easier for him to grasp objects. Experimentation with the hands is so exciting you will probably observe the young child holding something in both hands most of the time. Releasing is also a new skill the baby will need to practice.

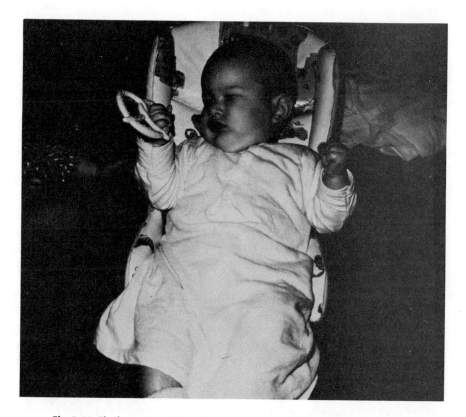

Fig. 5-10. The beginning of the object experiences phase is evidenced by grasping.

The following activities are examples of things you can do with the child to provide object experiences. These activities should not be viewed as an exhaustive list. They are just ideas to help you get started and to assist you in thinking about your child's developmental needs. We anticipate that you and the child will create many additional activities.

Activities to enhance object experiences
Objects, Objects, Objects

PURPOSES: (1) To stimulate reaching and grasping, (2) to stimulate visual tracking, and (3) to stimulate practice in coordinating vision and prehension.

MATERIALS: A variety of different objects that are safe for the child to explore. Include objects of different sizes, textures, and colors. Remember, the baby tends to put everything in her mouth, so be aware of the safety factor.

ACTIVITY: Suspend the objects at eye level. You may suspend them by attaching them loosely with clothespins, or by attaching them to strips of cloth and laying the cloth over a rope or elastic string across the infant's bed. Two essential considerations are that the child can easily see the objects and that she can pull it off the line and examine her prize. Change the objects often because the infant tires of them easily.

VARIATIONS:

1. Suspend objects that make interesting noises. Place them far enough from the baby so that she will have to reach to strike or grasp them. Also suspend them so she can kick at them.
2. Suspend various objects in different locations so that the baby will have to move her body to contact them.

Touch and Feel

PURPOSES: To provide opportunities for the infant to (1) experience using his sense of touch, (2) practice discriminating between the feelings evoked by touching different kinds of objects, (3) practice distinguishing between "me" and "not me," and (4) participate in a mutually enjoyable activity with another person.

MATERIALS: Small pieces of cloth with various textures such as velvet, flannel, suede, silk, wool, and plastic. You can also use stuffed animals covered with materials that differ in texture. Sew the pieces of material together to make a ball, octopus, doughnut, snake, or any other shape the baby can grab and hold onto. Stuff the object loosely so that the infant can grasp it with ease.

ACTIVITY: Give the stuffed toy to the infant and help him to discover the different textures. For example, you may need to take his hand and rub it across one kind of material on the cloth toy. As you do so, talk to the baby about how it feels. You can say, "Feel how soft." You don't have to use those exact words. The idea is to give the infant experiences with different kinds of feelings and to provide the words that describe the sensations at the same time. You may think the baby is too young to understand the words; thus you may not bother to talk to the baby. However, he will enjoy hearing the words, and children learn to understand and to use language through *repeated* experiences in which words, objects, and actions are associated.

Ball Games

PURPOSE: To develop the hand-eye coordination necessary for prehension.

MATERIALS: Balls or other rolling objects that differ in size and color.

ACTIVITY: Roll the ball to the baby and encourage her to watch it and grab it when it gets near enough. Be sure to allow plenty of time for the child to examine and manipulate the ball after she gains control of it.

Book Game

PURPOSE: To stimulate the infant to imitate pointing, reaching, and page-turning movements and to encourage him to respond vocally if he so desires.

MATERIALS: A book with large pictures.

ACTIVITY: Point to various aspects of the pictures while describing the actions or feelings they portray. Slowly turn the pages, being sure the infant is paying attention to your actions. Encourage the baby to respond by moving and making sounds.

Follow the Object

PURPOSES: (1) To stimulate the infant to visually locate and track a moving object by lifting her head, and (2) to develop strength in the upper body muscles that will be used in sitting.

MATERIALS: Any object that interests the child.

ACTIVITY: Stand beside the infant while she is lying on her back in bed or kneel beside her while she is lying on the floor. Hold the toy in front of the infant within her visual range. Encourage the infant to find the object by talking to her and by moving or shaking the object. When the infant finds the object, hold it close to her and slowly wave it downward toward her feet. If you do this, she will have to lift her head to follow the movement of the toy. Repeat the activity, but do not tire the baby. Remember to provide verbal information and encouragement throughout the activity.

Strike the Pans

PURPOSES: (1) To stimulate arm movement, (2) to develop hand-eye coordination, and (3) to provide an activity that develops coordination and an awareness of the body's midline by having the baby bring both of his arms together in front of the body.

MATERIALS: Two foil pie pans or plastic plates.

ACTIVITY: While the infant is watching you, strike the pans together and say "Wham-wham-wham," or any other appropriate sound. Then give the baby the pans and encourage him to imitate your actions. It may be necessary for you to guide the infant through the action by moving his arms. Continue to verbalize the sound as the infant strikes the pans together, and enthusiastically encourage him to continue, but don't tire him.

VARIATION: Progress to having the baby play pat-a-cake by imitating your hand clapping.

Cover-up

PURPOSE: To assist the child in developing the concepts of object reality and object permanence.

MATERIALS: An interesting object and a cloth diaper, napkin, or small blanket.

ACTIVITY: This activity resembles the game of peek-a-boo with some extensions and variations. Place the cloth over your face saying, "Where's Mommy?" Then say, "There she is," and remove the cloth. Repeat this and then try the following variations. Place the cloth over the infant's face saying, "Where's Jamey?" Then remove the cloth and say "There he is," (or "Boo.") Repeat the activity while encouraging the baby to remove the cloth himself. Give the baby a great deal of positive reinforcement.

VARIATION: Substitute a toy for your face. Cover the toy and say, "Where is the car?" Remove the cover and say, "There's the car!" Repeat this several times; then try to get the baby to remove the cloth or pick up the car. An infant at this age will probably not find the car if it is completely hidden, so only partially cover the object. Then as the baby's perception develops, you can increase the amount of the toy you cover until it is entirely covered.

Touch and Name

PURPOSES: (1) To stimulate development of the concept of "me" versus "not me," (2) to develop an awareness of different body parts, and (3) to assist the infant in making associations between words, objects, and actions.

MATERIALS: None.

ACTIVITY: Touch different parts of your infant's body as you name them. "This is Jamey's leg. Here is Jamey's hand. Where's Jamey's nose? Here it is!" Also touch and name your own body parts. For example, "Here's Mommy's nose. Here's Daddy's nose. Here's Jamey's nose." Even though your baby won't use these words himself for some time, he is learning. Through this type of experience, he is beginning to recognize the words and to associate them with things in the environment.

VARIATION: Once your child begins to learn the names of body parts, try turning the game around and ask, for example, "Where's Jamey's leg? Where's Mommy's arm? Where's the dolly's nose?" Encourage the child to point to the body part.

Twist, Creep, Flop, Crawl

PURPOSE: To provide the physical exercise necessary for the development of movement skills.

MATERIALS: None.

ACTIVITY: Begin by getting on the floor with your infant. Place an object across the room and encourage the baby to get it. As the baby begins to move, imitate her movement patterns. If the baby stops initiating her own movements and looks to you for ideas, create some patterns that are similar to but just a little different from the baby's own.

VARIATION: Vary the type of object the baby must retrieve and the direction and distance she must move.

Stand and Play

PURPOSE: To stimulate the baby to practice getting up and down and maintaining a standing position.

MATERIALS: A very low table that provides a place for the baby to hold onto.

ACTIVITY: Place a few objects on the table within the baby's reach. Encourage him to hold onto the table with one hand and manipulate the objects with the other. Repeat the game, using a different group of objects.

Mirror Game

PURPOSES: (1) To increase the infant's self-awareness, (2) to stimulate awareness of different sides of the body, and (3) to assist the baby in making the association between her own movements and those of the mirror image.

MATERIALS: A mirror positioned so that the infant can safely sit in front of it.

ACTIVITY: Place the baby in a sitting position in front of the mirror and, if necessary, encourage her to move, gesture, and make different facial expressions. The baby may do all of this alone; if so, you can just stand back and enjoy it all.

Get the Ball

PURPOSE: To stimulate the infant to locate an object in space and to move to obtain it.

MATERIALS: A rubber ball at least 5 inches in diameter.

ACTIVITY: Sit on the floor about 5 feet in front of the baby. Bounce the ball while saying, "Jamey, get the ball; come on, get the ball," or something of a similar nature. When the baby gets to the ball, grasps it, and brings it close to his body, praise him verbally and nonverbally. Repeat the activity, but *don't* tire the infant.

Pick Up What I Drop

PURPOSES: To practice (1) the skill of dropping, and (2) visually tracking an object and relocating it after it has moved out of the immediate visual field.

MATERIALS: Small objects the baby can grasp.

ACTIVITY: Put the infant in a high chair or some type of seat. Hand her an object and let her manipulate and drop it. Pick up the object and hand it back to the baby. Encourage the baby to visually track the movement of the object by saying something like, "Where did the bear go?" or "Where is Tanya's bear?" Repeat the activity over and over using different objects. You will probably tire of the activity long before the baby does, but if you focus on her pleasure and learning, you will be able to patiently endure the monotony of your role in the activity.

VARIATION: When the infant is able to maintain a standing position, she can drop her own object and then bend down to pick it up. You may need to guide the activity and assist the infant in picking up the object, and you must reinforce her efforts enthusiastically. The baby experiences a lot of frustration at times and needs to be comforted and encouraged.

THE SPACE EXPERIENCES PHASE

The space experiences phase (8 to 12 months) is a continuation and extension of the sensory and object experiences phases. During the phase of object experiences (4 to 8 months), the infant develops the ability to relate to objects as they exist in space. The two essential components of this ability are the infant's awareness of object permanence and the awareness that he can effect change by acting on objects. The development of these awarenesses sets the stage for the emergence of the space experiences phase, which is the ability to associate one object to another and to establish a relationship between them. The infant's sensory abilities continue to become more refined. The awareness of the self as an object among other objects continues to increase, as does the awareness of object permanence. It may help you to envision this developmental sequence if you think of it as a jigsaw puzzle that the infant is gradually putting together. As she practices and experiences, she is fitting pieces of the puzzle together. Each new piece added creates a more complete picture and, as a result, the picture is constantly changing and enlarging.

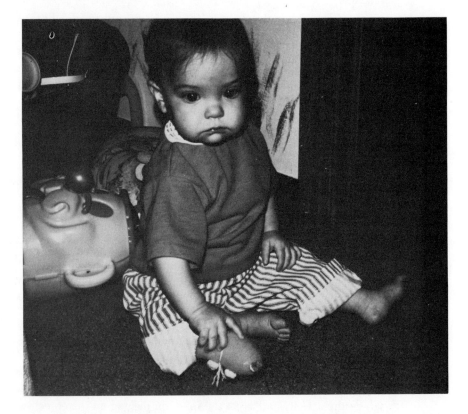

Fig. 5-11. During the space experiences phase the infant becomes aware of the ability to effect change by acting on objects.

After the tremendous surge of motor activity necessary in practicing the physical skills that emerge in the object experiences phase, there is a temporary "slowing down." The infant's ability to sit up is now refined, and standing up and getting down become easier tasks. The ability to maintain a standing position frees the child to readily use the hands. It also results in a different perspective of the world because many of the things that were hidden in a sitting position now come into view.

During the space experiences phase, the infant's memory and ability to make associations markedly improves. The infant is now capable of keeping a series of ideas in mind. This new capability is accompanied by a distinct change in behavior. The infant now becomes bored with repetitions of the same stimulus and demands variety. When the infant was younger, the same stimulus occurring over and over would continue to hold his interest; just the action of the object provided sufficient stimulation. But now the infant needs continuous change. He is capable of associating cause with effect. Now it is necessary to provide the infant with a variety of opportunities to observe things happening. He wants to see where an object goes when he drops it and what happens to the toy truck when he pushes it. In other words, he needs to be able to see what his actions (the cause) do to the object (the effect).

Forming associations by relating one object to another is a gradual process. The child will begin by displaying the ability to pick up and manipulate two objects, one in each hand. Then she will progress to relating these objects by striking them together, holding them close together, dropping one and then the other, or dropping them both at the same time. She may drop one of the objects she has been holding and pick up a third, or she may put one of the objects in her mouth and then pick up another one. From the beginning of this new phase, the child embarks on a long and intensive study concerning the displacement of objects and simple cause-and-effect relationships.

It is fascinating to watch an infant study the properties of objects. He will rotate and turn an object, move it back and forth in front of his face or twist and turn his head to look at it. The infant continues to learn about the properties of objects by participating in activities such as crumpling a paper, rattling boxes, listening to a watch tick, or pointing, poking, touching, and prying with his extended index finger. By performing these activities, the child is discovering size constancy and is discovering that things have a bottom and a top. You can provide practice relative to this concept by handing the infant objects with the bottom facing him. For example, hand the child a bottle with the bottom facing him and the nipple pointing away. If he turns the bottle around and begins to suck, he is displaying knowledge of this concept. Allow plenty of time for him to figure out a solution, but if he screams in frustration, help him.

At the same time the infant is learning concepts of size perception, he is also learning depth perception. You can test the infant's ability to detect near

Fig. 5-12. Infants study objects intently and will move through space to explore an interesting object.

and far by handing him an object. Stand so you are well out of reach of your child and see if he will grab for the object when you extend it toward him. If he does not reach for it, move within reach of the child and hand him the object. If he grabs it within reach, but doesn't attempt to reach out for it when it is out of reach, you will know his depth perception has developed. You can also evaluate this ability by handing the child a large object (for example, a large ball). If he is aware of size, he will reach with two hands toward a large object and, conversely, will reach with only one hand if the object is small. This activity will demonstrate whether or not the child has reached the developmental milestone of determining the size of objects and their location in space relative to himself.

The infant's growing awareness of object permanence now enables her to search for a hidden object *if she sees you hide it*. This new ability offers an opportunity for many fun hide-and-seek games. For example, you can hide a toy while the infant watches you. You can hide it under a diaper, napkin, pillow, or in a container. Watch the excitement of your infant when she locates the missing object. Pay attention to the way she communicates

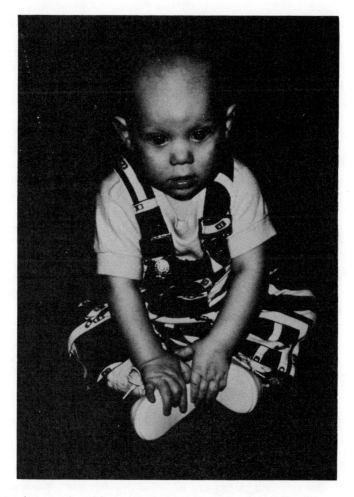

Fig. 5-13. Infants watch and listen intently, always ready to imitate the actions and sounds around them.

the message, "Let's play again." This communication will not only indicate the extent of her language development but will also indicate the child's understanding of cause-and-effect relationships. When the child becomes acquainted with the game as you originally played it, make it more difficult by adding another dimension. With the child watching, hide the object under a diaper or small blanket, then remove the object and put it under a pillow. Make sure the child observes your actions. Then challenge the child to find the toy. Depending on the level of your infant's development, she may locate the object, or she may look under the blanket (the place she found it before). If the child is successful, try using three different hiding places. Put the object in one place, then another, and then hide it in a third place. Be sure the child is watching the entire time. Just for fun you may want to try the same activities with your pet dog. Infants love to watch a dog play the game. And you may discover that the infant will initiate the game with the dog. Moving an object from one location to another is called *object displacement*. Challenging a child by using object displacement provides an opportunity for many fun-filled activities because of the variety of objects and hiding places you can utilize.

During this phase much of the child's learning involves imitation. The infant has been imitating since shortly after birth, but imitative actions are much more noticeable now. Infants are not selective imitators. That is, they don't select what they will imitate, but rather they imitate everything. Therefore you are a constant model for the infant. This means that if the child is having trouble with a certain task, you can assist by being a model. As the child watches how you solve the problem, learning through imitation will occur.

By the end of their first year, most children have constructed a basic reality of the world around them. They are capable of spatially locating things in relation to themselves. They can execute a wide range of purposeful movement patterns and form associations between the way they move (the cause) and the action of an object (the effect).

The following activities are designed to guide you in assisting the infant's development of spatial awareness. Again, we anticipate that you will use these as suggestions and will be stimulated to create a variety of original activities.

Activities to develop spatial awareness
String Games

PURPOSES: (1) To enable the child to practice *action solving*, a skill prerequisite to problem solving, (2) to provide practice using the fingers and thumb in a pincer grasp, (3) to develop hand-eye coordination, (4) to assist in developing cause-and-effect relationships and relating objects to each other in space, and (5) to practice remembering the location of a toy with the toy in view and with the toy hidden.

MATERIALS: A piece of string that is attached to a toy, a piece of cloth, various toys and play objects that can be used as funnels such as shoe boxes, toilet paper rolls, paper towel rolls, and coffee cans that have both ends removed.

ACTIVITY: Begin with a cloth placed on the floor in front of the child. Put a toy under the end of the cloth. See if the child will pull the cloth off from the toy so he can find it. If the child seems unable to comprehend the purpose of the game, demonstrate the activity while verbalizing what is happening. It is more interesting if you use playful language. For example, if the toy under the cloth is a car, you can say, "Here comes the red car; beep, beep, look out!" Or if the toy is an animal you can say, "Here comes the dog; bark, bark." When the child completes the task and finds the toy, give him time to study the object. You may want to discuss the parts of the car or the body parts of the dog if you can maintain the child's attention.

Once the child has mastered this game, you can make the activity more challenging by using a string or rope attached to an object. This makes the activity more difficult because the string is smaller than the object, and therefore the child must grasp it with finger and thumb opposition rather than with the whole hand.

VARIATIONS:

1. Pull on the string to make the object pass through "tunnels" ranging in size from the space under a chair to the space inside the cardboard toilet paper tube.

2. Place a piece of cloth over the opening of the "tunnel" so the object cannot be seen until it is pulled through the covered opening.

3. Use several strings but attach a toy to only one of them. Ask the child to pull the toy toward himself. If he pulls a string with no toy on it say, "There's no toy coming through on that string." When he pulls the right string say, "Look, here comes the toy!"

4. The following is the most difficult of the string games and requires some extra materials. Get a fairly large cardboard box from the grocery store. Cut three openings out of the bottom of the box. Tape a cloth over each opening to cover it. Place the box on its side with the bottom facing the child. Sit behind the box and have the child sit on the other side. Make sure he cannot see inside the box. Put three strings through the openings of the box, one coming out of each door. Put different objects on the strings and have the child pull on the strings to obtain the objects. Next put objects only on the middle string. Have the child pull on the strings. See if he can figure out which string is attached to an object. Change the position of the string with the toy on it. You may want to color code the string, for example, red could mean there is a toy on the string. Have the red string always attached to the toy, regardless of location.

Find the Toy

PURPOSES: (1) To assist the child in developing the concept that objects continue to exist even though they are out of sight (object permanence), (2) to develop visual memory by requiring the child to follow the path of an object and a sequence of events, and (3) to assist the child in relating the source of a sound with the location of an object.

MATERIALS: A variety of toys that make sounds (such as bells, squeeze toys, rattles, or blocks inside plastic cups).

ACTIVITY: Use an object that makes a sound (such as a bell). Shake the bell in front of the child until the child notices its location. Move the object around in front of the child so she can visually track the object with the aid of the auditory clue. When you are sure you have the child's attention, hide the object under a piece of furniture or behind your back. Keep ringing the bell because this gives the child constant auditory clues and encourages the child to continue searching for the toy. As you continue playing the game, hide the toy in the same location so the child can be repeatedly successful in finding it. Then, progress to hiding it in different locations.

Play the game using a block and two cups. Put the block under one cup as the child watches. Slide the cup back and forth with the block under it to create a sound that will provide auditory clues. Also slide the other cups so the child can see and hear that there is no sound coming from the empty cup. Ask the child to find the block.

Repeat these activities, using objects that do make sounds. This removes the auditory clues, thereby requiring the child to locate the toy purely on the basis of visual cues.

Hide-and-Seek Games

PURPOSE: To practice using auditory and visual cues to locate an object in space.

MATERIALS: The home or day-care environment.

ACTIVITY: This activity is for the increasingly mobile child and can be modified for the not-so-mobile child. It resembles the "find the toy" game previously described. In the game, you hide and encourage the child to come and find you. At first, you will need to give the child auditory cues by continuously saying, "Where am I? Come and get me." Visual cues are also necessary, so you need to continuously pop in and out of the hiding place. When the child finds you, make sure there is a warm interaction between the two of you so the child will be reinforced.

VARIATION: A variation of this game is to add the peek-a-boo technique. You can hide behind a door or chair and pop out saying, "Peek-a-boo; I see you."

Mirror Games—"It's Me"

PURPOSE: To develop the concepts that are prerequisite to the development of *laterality* (the concept of left and right sides of the body) and the spatial relationships of up and down and near and far.

MATERIALS: A box containing interesting toys such as stuffed animals, dolls, hats, sunglasses, wigs, and so on and a full-length mirror that is the baby's height. (An adult full-length mirror placed on its side is ideal.)

ACTIVITIES: Have the child sit in front of the mirror, and encourage him to move his body parts in various ways. When the child appears to have run out of ideas, try the following:

1. Repeat the mirror game on p. 69 while the child observes his actions reflected in the mirror.
2. Remove one of the objects from the toy box or let the child select one. Use the object to stimulate actions. For example, take a hat or

wig out of the box and put it on the child's head. Ask the child, "Who is that in the mirror? Is that Andy? Where's Mommy?" Repeat, using other objects.

3. While sitting behind the child, make different motions. See if the child turns around to look at you, then turns back to look in the mirror, and then looks back at you.

4. Sit beside the child and play pat-a-cake with your mirror image and see if the child will imitate your actions.

5. Using the stuffed animals and dolls, you can play the "body parts games" (p. 85). Touch and name the parts of the toy's body. Encourage the child to touch the toy's body parts on the mirror reflection.

6. Pull a ball or a rolling toy such as a car out of the box. Roll the ball or car toward the mirror saying, "Here it comes; can you see it in the mirror?" Then roll the ball away from the mirror. Repeat this several times while checking to see if the child is tracking the mirror image. Then leave the ball or car with the child and see what he does to explore the toy's movement possibilities.

Reading Games

PURPOSES: (1) To provide activities for the child to begin associating experience and language and (2) to stimulate different sense modalities.

MATERIALS: Homemade books containing photographs or pictures from magazines or newspapers or books made from outdoor objects such as leaves, sticks, dirt, rocks, and other collectibles. You can also use picture books that have been commercially printed.

ACTIVITY: The activity begins with making the books. The child should be involved in this process from the beginning. First the two of you must collect a variety of objects. You may want to divide them into indoor and outdoor objects. Next mount your treasures on construction paper or cloth. Then simply punch holes in one side or in the top of the pages and tie them together with yarn. You may want to leave some pages blank so the child can color on these and make her own pictures.

Let her turn the pages, stopping whenever she chooses. *Don't* try to *make* her read like an adult, going through the book page by page. Young children aren't interested in that type of reading, so just let her explore the book.

Continually verbalize while the child explores. If there is a picture of an object that is in the room, point it out to help the child make a relationship between the real object and the picture of the object.

Rolling Along

PURPOSES: (1) To provide practice in visual tracking, hand-eye coordination, and body coordination and (2) to enable the child to experience and explore different types of sensory stimulation.

MATERIALS: Balls of various sizes (large ones are easier to maneuver), toys that roll, or cylinders of any type such as covered orange juice cans or coffee cans. You may want to cover the cans with different textures such as carpet, sandpaper, tape, or cloth. You may also want to put noisemakers inside or spray the outside with perfume scented deodorants or some other scent. The possibilities are limitless.

ACTIVITY: Roll a brightly colored ball (or some other object) close to the child, encouraging her to move to obtain it. If you repeat this activity or if you roll the ball too far away from the child, you may find that she becomes distracted by other interesting objects in the environment. If this happens, just let her explore the new source of stimulation. Then when she is ready, return to the rolling game. Another problem may be that the child does not want to give up the object she has retrieved. If this happens, just let her keep it. When she seems ready to continue with the game, you can introduce a different rolling object.

VARIATIONS: Add variety by using different kinds of rolling objects such as those listed above as materials. Attaching photographs or other pictures to a ball provides a new interest. Wrapping masking tape around the ball is also a good idea. The child enjoys pulling it off and it provides excellent practice in the use of finger and thumb opposition. Be creative! Look around the house and select anything that can safely be used as a rolling object.

Fig. 5-14. A photograph attached to a ball creates a novel play object.

Give-away and Take-away games

PURPOSES: (1) To provide practice of the pincer grasp (thumb and finger opposition), (2) to practice releasing the grasp of an object, and (3) to practice language skills.

MATERIALS: Any object that can be safely held in one of the child's hands.

ACTIVITIES: Hand the child an object such as a small ball. While you are giving it to the child say, "Here is the ball." After the child explores the ball, ask him to give it back to you. When he hands it to you say, "Thank you." Then hand it back to the child, encouraging him to say, "Thank you." Repeat the game, using various objects. You can, for example, play the game at mealtime, by asking the child to hand his spoon, bowl, cup, or bottle, to you; you should then thank him when you receive each object.

When the child has mastered the concept of "thank you," you can introduce the concepts of "please" and "you're welcome."

Water and Sand Activities

PURPOSES: (1) To practice hand-eye coordination and (2) to enable the child to explore and experience different types of sensory stimulation.

MATERIALS: Water, sand, plastic scoops, wooden spoons, plastic squeeze bottles, containers of various sizes, plastic shovels, corks from wine bottles, commercial floating toys and sand toys, ice cubes, food coloring, or bubble bath. Use your imagination.

ACTIVITIES: Sand and water play are messy activities, but some preplanning can cut down on the mess. If you are inside, you can put down a sheet of plastic to catch the spills. You can also limit the amount of water or sand used. Provide enough water for splashing but not enough to make a mess. Allow the child time to explore freely. Here are some suggestions you can use when you think that additional stimulation is needed.

Water activity suggestions

1. Provide various objects for filling, pouring, and emptying.
2. Put some ice cubes in the water. Watch the child carefully when the cubes become small enough to fit into her mouth because she could choke on them.
3. Adding food coloring is fun. Children enjoy watching the water change colors.
4. Put bubble bath in the water and encourage the child to splash, causing bubbles to form.

Sand activity suggestions

1. Provide various objects for filling, emptying, and pouring.
2. Provide various digging utensils. The child may eat the sand, so be observant. (You may want to use cereal such as cornmeal or Cream of

Wheat instead of sand, to avoid worrying that the child might eat the sand.)

3. Provide small cars and trucks to travel through the sand or cereal.
4. Cans with holes in the bottom are fun (or use sifters or strainers). Children enjoy watching cereal or sand fall through the holes or the screen.

Painting Activities

PURPOSES: (1) To develop hand-eye coordination, (2) to enable the child to explore and experience the sensory stimulation of different colors, textures, and tastes, (3) to enable the child to perceive that he can bring about change, and (4) to enable the child to form the associations that will assist him in developing cause-and-effect relationships.

MATERIALS: Edibles such as mayonnaise, mustard, soy sauce, beet juice, or a prepared starch or flour base with something added to color it; paper for painting, old clothes, and brushes (such as shortened paintbrushes, cottonswabs, toothbrushes, or sponges). Objects used as stamps can add an extra dimension to the painting. These might include plastic cups, old puzzle pieces, or potatoes cut at one end and incised with designs, corks, cucumbers, or green peppers. The list is endless, so just use your imagination.

ACTIVITIES: Prepare a working space for the child, keeping in mind the mess he will create. Tape the paper to a work surface and provide the painting materials (edibles such as mayonnaise, mustard, soy sauce, beet juice, or a prepared starch or flour base with something added to color it). Then just let the child explore. At first, he may just play in the "paint," squeezing it through his fingers, tasting it, smelling it, and rubbing it on his body. Give the child plenty of time to explore. If the child seems to have run out of ideas, you may need to show him some finger-painting techniques.

After the child has explored finger painting, you can progress to brush painting and stamp painting. Stamp painting is easier because it involves up-and-down hand motions, rather than straight and circular brush strokes.

Follow Me

PURPOSES: (1) To practice crawling skills and (2) to develop spatial awareness concepts such as up and down, in and out, through, around, over, and under.

MATERIALS: Furniture, structures, or play objects that can be arranged to create various spaces and pathways.

ACTIVITIES: Model various crawling activities, encouraging the child to follow you. Include crawling inside a box, through a tunnel, up and down steps and inclines, under improvised bridges, over low objects, and around chairs or larger toys. Enthusiastically verbalize your actions and be sure to maintain a playful attitude.

Copycat Games

PURPOSE: To develop the ability to pay attention to visual stimuli and to imitate the actions of another person.

MATERIALS: Common household objects.

ACTIVITIES: Children like to imitate, so the child should catch on fast, especially if you start the game by imitating an action the child is doing. Be sure to verbalize concerning your actions.

1. Touch different parts of your body and see if the child will imitate by touching her corresponding parts.
2. Crawl around on the floor, and have the child imitate as you go under a table, around objects, and up and then down a few stairs.
3. Make different faces and see if the child can imitate them. Stick out your tongue. Touch and then hold your tongue with your hand. Encourage the child's attempts to touch and grasp her tongue.
4. Make different vocal noises such as animal sounds. You may want to add pictures from books or photographs to increase the excitement of this game.
5. Put on a hat; then take it off and set it down. See if the child picks it up and puts it on her head. Repeat, increasing the speed of putting

Fig. 5-15. The ability to pay attention to visual stimuli and to imitate the actions of another person are foundation skills for the later skill of "action" solving.

on and taking off the hat and see if the child detects the speed change and imitates by increasing her speed.

6. Have the child imitate you as you open and close your hands, your eyes, and your mouth, and as you move your head, arms, and legs up and down or from side to side.

7. Pretend you are drinking from a cup, eating from a spoon, folding a diaper, washing dishes, or performing other activities of daily living and see if the child will imitate your actions.

8. Stand up and sit down, challenging the child to imitate. If the child can stand, do a series of movements such as standing—squatting—standing or squatting—standing—squatting.

9. Hold a ball or a similar object and give the child one too. Hold it up over your head, out to the side, behind your back, or roll it down your legs. See if the child can imitate your actions.

THE PERSISTENCE PHASE

We have designated the final phase of infant development as persistence. We selected this term to emphasize that now the child's actions are not only purposeful, but they are also persistent. By being persistent, the child continues to work and experiment until discovering some kind of answer. Pre-

Fig. 5-16. As children develop they become more purposeful and persistent in their actions.

viously the child had been putting together the bits and pieces of reality. In this final phase the infant completes a large portion of the jigsaw puzzle. The infant is now capable of experiencing reality in a way that will expand self-awareness as well as awareness of the environment.

When the infant becomes capable of associating sensory stimulation with objects and relating objects to spaces, many new behavioral activities emerge. For example, development of the ability to relate a container to what it contains stimulates many emptying and filling activities. The child realizes that if small objects are dropped into tin cans, various sounds will be produced. He realizes that when sand is put into a bucket, it will yield different weights, and when sand is poured out of a bucket, different shapes can be produced. He might place blocks in a tray and then dump them out just to see what happens. Anything that can be put into something else and then taken out again provides a fascinating learning activity for the child. Size and shape concepts are now being extended in ways that enable the child to reach conclusions such as, "It's too big to fit," or "This shape does not allow this object to go inside." Concepts relative to contrasting objects begin to emerge. For example, the child can now conclude that things which fit are the same and those which don't fit are different.

Stacking and knocking down become favorite pastimes for the child. You

Fig. 5-17. Containers and objects provide fascinating ways of learning about size and shape.

can observe that the child now creates and destroys with equal excitement. These kinds of activities involve more complex associations because they involve the concept of balancing objects one on top of another.

Cause-and-effect associations are growing as the self grows. The child is becoming more aware of himself as a causal agent among other causal agents. Now he realizes that he can put objects in positions to cause their own change. For example, a child may place a car at the top of an incline and watch it roll down or may put a ball at the top of a slide so it rolls downward of its own accord.

The child now becomes proficient at the game of object hide-and-seek. She is capable of finding an object after many visible displacements (after being moved from one place to another) and eventually becomes capable of finding an object with invisible displacement. The following activity is an example of invisible displacement. Enclose an object in your hand and place your closed hand under a piece of cloth; then remove your closed hand. The child will first look in your hand, but when the object is not there she will immediately look under the cloth.

The child in this stage not only is capable of playing object hide-and-seek games, but also finds total body hide-and-seek an exciting activity. The child, now aware of himself as distinct from other objects, begins relating this self to space and other people. For example, if you show the child an object and then hide it behind your back, the child will move around behind you and locate the object. A similar example occurs when the child is playing and loses control of a ball that rolls under the couch. The child will walk around behind the sofa to locate the ball.

The ability to symbolically represent events, objects, and people in the mind is the beginning of a new and exciting developmental phase. The child becomes capable of experiencing reality through insight. This enables him to experience the reality of space. For the first time, he can conceive of space as a motionless environment in which his body and other objects are located.

The ability to symbolically represent actions markedly affects the child's conception causality. The child can now utilize representation to infer a cause given only its effect and, in turn, can foresee an effect given only its cause. These mental milestones are accompanied by physical milestones, and the two are inseparably interwoven. For example, the infant's visual potential is greatly increased when she becomes capable of sitting up and freely turning her head. The ability to maintain a sitting position frees the hands to reach out farther and in different directions. Then when the infant learns to walk, a whole new spatial world opens up to her. Thus at the same time children are learning to move, they are also learning by moving. You can observe this relationship by noting that as mobility increases, the amount and variety of cognitive stimulation available to them also increases.

The onset of the persistence phase is usually paralleled by the desire to begin walking. Walking indicates the beginning of a new developmental stage because in addition to markedly enlarging the child's sensory world, it frees the child's hands from the restrictions imposed by crawling. The child also becomes increasingly independent in this stage. Of course, the desire to function as a distinct and separate individual naturally emerges in combination with persistence and the ability to freely move about in the environment.

As the child experiments with standing and the beginning stages of walking, he may discover other new skills. For example, if the child loses his balance and topples forward, he may discover a new way of crawling on the hands and feet. This may lead him to discover that crawling on the hands and feet is a faster form of locomotion than crawling on the hands and knees.

Two other skills that commonly emerge from the child's ability to stand are squatting and stooping. The infant will deliberately drop toys just to squat down and pick them up. These two skills evidence the infant's increasing interest in exploring depth and distance. Children may drop objects with one hand and then the other to experiment with the sensation of doing the same thing with different sides of the body. This evidences the relationship of body and spatial awareness. The development of the ability to execute movements with one hand or one foot and then the other, as well as the ability to use different body parts, is paralleled by discoveries of different ways to move objects through space.

The infant's first unsupported walking steps are often accidental. These frequently occur when she is trying to reach for something just out of reach. With practice the infant soon learns how to maintain a balanced body position while stepping, how to turn around, and how to stop. An interesting correlate to walking is swimming. Pay attention to the infant's skills in the bathtub; when the child begins walking, chances are you will also see swimming motions.

There are two very important things for you to keep in mind during this stage of the child's development. First, you should remember that development is an individual matter and that all children will not respond in the same way. Second, when a child begins upright locomotion, a period of adjustment to this vertical world is necessary. Children may express caution and fear as they begin to adapt to this "new approach" to life. As always, warmth, understanding, and encouragement are essential to assist the child in attaining this developmental milestone. The following activities are designed as suggestions to assist you to effectively function as a caregiver.

Activities to enhance development during the persistence phase
Body Parts Games
Where is your hand

PURPOSES: (1) To assist the child in recognizing the names of different body parts and (2) to enable the child to form associations between (a) the name and the location of body parts and (b) the name and the actions of body parts.

MATERIALS: None.

ACTIVITY: Name one of the child's principal body parts and ask her to locate it. You may say, "Show me Leslie's hand," or "Where is Leslie's hand?" Continue the game by naming parts such as the arm, foot, leg, or head. If the child readily responds, you can progress to less prominent body parts such as the shoulder, elbow, or knee. As an added element, you can also have the child point to the body parts. And you can include body parts the child cannot see, such as her ears, nose, mouth, eyes, or teeth.

You can vary the game in many different ways by adding action words. Ask the child to rub, shake, or wiggle her hands, feet, fingers, or toes. The following list indicates various body parts and body actions that can be combined to provide challenging learning activities.

Body parts	Body actions
Hands	Reach
Feet	Point
Legs	Touch
Arms	Grasp
Knees	Rub
Elbows	Pat
Head	Wiggle
Back	Clap
Shoulders	Stretch
Fingers	Bend
Toes	Shake
Thumbs	Wave
Nose	
Mouth	
Eyes	
Ears	

Where is the dolly's nose

PURPOSES: (1) To reinforce the association of the names and locations of body parts and (2) to assist the child to form associations concerning the similarity of his own body parts and the body parts of other people, animals, and toys.

MATERIALS: A doll, stuffed toys, animals, and pictures of these materials.

ACTIVITY: Name different body parts, challenging the child to touch the part of his body you name. Progress to asking, "Where is Daddy's hand?" You can then continue by naming other body parts. Substitute a doll, a stuffed animal, or a real animal. Finally, show the child large pictures of people or animals, asking him to identify various parts of the bodies. A

Fig. 5-18. Body parts games become more complex when the child is asked to relate the location of his body parts to the location of the same part of an object in the shape of a body.

new dimension can be added to the game by having the child name a body part and then touching that part of your body.

Relating body parts

PURPOSES: (1) To enable the child to associate the name and location of one body part with the name and location of another body part and (2) to assist the child in spatially relating one body part to another.

MATERIALS: None.

ACTIVITY: This is an imitation activity. In this activity, tell the child to put one body part on another while you perform the action as the child watches and imitates. Some examples are, "Put your hand on your head,"

"Put your elbow on your foot," "Put your nose on your knee," "Put your ear on your foot," and "Put your hand on your shoulder."

When the child evidences the ability to relate her body parts to each other, you can progress to combining body parts with objects. For example, ask the child to put her nose on the floor, her ear on the table, her knee on the floor, or her head on the couch. Combine any body part with any object. Begin by using the spatial relationship *on*, and if the child progresses rapidly, try the relationship *under*. You might say, for example, "Put your hand under the table," "Put your leg under the chair," or "Put your head under the chair."

Body positions

PURPOSES: (1) To enable the child to recognize different body positions and (2) to assist the child in associating the names of body parts with positions.

MATERIALS: None.

ACTIVITY: Using the modeling teaching method, assume the following positions while encouraging the child to imitate your actions.

1. Sit down on your bottom.
2. Stand up on your feet.
3. Kneel on your knees.
4. Squat down on your feet.
5. Get on your hands and knees.
6. Get on your hands and feet.
7. Lie on your back.
8. Lie on your front.
9. Stand on one foot. (This is very difficult, and the child will probably find something to hold onto while executing it. You can assist by offering your hand or arm as a support.)
10. When the child becomes aware of these positions and is able to control his body in a balanced position, you may want to add locomotor movements. You might say, for example, "Let's kneel and walk on our knees; see how short we are"; "Let's get down on our hands and knees and crawl"; or "Let's walk on our hands and feet."

What's missing

PURPOSE: To enable the child to associate the location and appearance of facial features.

MATERIALS: Paper plates or cardboard in the shape of a head or body, crayons or dry markers, construction paper or a felt board, scissors, and tape or glue.

ACTIVITY: Make the shape of a head out of a paper plate and color some hair on top. Cut facial features, such as the eyes, ears, nose, and mouth out of construction paper. Sit down with the child and put the parts on the face, verbalizing what you are doing. Make reference to your own face and the child's face. Attach the parts to the head by using tape or glue. Put all the parts on the head except one and ask the child, "What's missing?" Assist the child with the answer if she does not know it. Give the body part to the child and see if she can put it in the correct place. This is a difficult activity, so if the child is repeatedly unsuccessful or becomes bored, put the game away and try it again in a few weeks.

An extension of this game is to make a felt body or body shape out of cardboard. Then after you have attached the facial features, you can cut out clothing and dress your "friend." You may want to include hats, shirts (long and short sleeve), pants (long and short), dresses, skirts, bathing suits, boots and other shoes, gloves and mittens, pockets, buttons, or zippers. As you dress your "friend," discuss things that might cause you to dress a certain way. For example, "What would you wear if it was real cold outside—long pants or short pants?" "What would you wear to go swimming?"

Puzzles

PURPOSES: (1) To develop manual dexterity and hand-eye coordination and (2) to develop shape recognition and the ability to associate shapes with matching spaces.

MATERIALS: Simple puzzles, either homemade or commercially manufactured.

ACTIVITIES: Begin with a one-piece or two-piece puzzle consisting of geometric shapes such as matching squares, rectangles, triangles, or circles. You may want to attach handles or knobs to the pieces so the child can easily grasp them. Let the child experiment with the pieces. If he does not discover the idea behind putting together and taking apart a puzzle, demonstrate while verbalizing your actions. When the child becomes more experienced, he will enjoy simple jigsaw puzzles. Jigsaw puzzles require that the child put together several parts to make a whole. Excellent wooden ones are produced commercially. You can also make them yourself.

Matching Games

PURPOSES: (1) To assist the child in associating real objects with pictures of objects, (2) to practice associating a name with an object, and (3) to stimulate color recognition.

MATERIALS: Pictures of objects that are available in the home, such as spoons, forks, cups, balls, chains, coat hangers, toothbrushes, dishrags, dolls, trucks, or flowers.

ACTIVITY: Locate as many pictures or photographs as possible from magazines or books. You may want to remove them from the original source and glue the picture on a sturdy piece of cardboard. Show the child the picture and ask, "What is this?" If the child responds, reinforce the effort even if the response is incorrect. Then say, "It's a red toothbrush. Can

Fig. 5-19. Puzzles develop shape recognition and the ability to associate shapes with matching spaces.

you find a real red toothbrush, so I can brush my teeth?" Reinforce the child by saying something like, "That's really good; you are so smart." Repeat the game using different pictures and the objects they portray.

A more challenging variation of this game is picture matching and object matching. For object matching, provide two or three sets of objects. For example, use two red cups, two blue toothbrushes, and two mittens. When the child picks up one object, ask him to find one just like the one he is holding. For example, if the child picks up a cup, ask him to find another cup for you so you can both have one. Reinforce the child, even if he picks up another object by saying, "Oh, you found a toothbrush; that is good. I'll see if I can find the other cup; here it is." If you continue to repeat this game in a relaxed manner, the child will soon catch on. Then you can progress to using sets of pictures instead of sets of objects.

Sorting Games

PURPOSES: (1) To enable the child to recognize and to identify certain colors, shapes, and sizes and (2) to enable the child to form associations between similar colors, shapes, and sizes.

MATERIALS: Four red balls, four blue balls, a red box, a blue box, toys of similar color, shape, or size.

ACTIVITIES: Begin with a sorting activity. For example, you can give the child four red balls, four blue balls, a red box, and a blue box. Ask the child to put the red balls in the red box and the blue balls in the blue box. Reinforce the child's efforts. If she is unable to sort the balls, cheerfully and playfully assist her. If the child is able to detect similarities and differences, you can progress to having her sort toys that are similar such as blocks, dolls, trucks, or puzzles. You can make cleanup activities learning experiences by placing one object on a shelf and asking the child to place all similar objects on the shelf with it. You can designate one section of the shelf for each type of toy. You may want to attach one toy of each kind to the shelf so it cannot be removed and therefore will serve as a guide to the child whenever cleanup time comes. As soon as the child is able to form an association between a real object and a picture of the object, you can attach pictures to the shelves to indicate where certain toys should be placed. The child will probably need to model your behavior at first, but soon will become self-directing if you provide enough encouragement and reinforcement. If you maintain a cheerful attitude and approach, and treat cleanup as a playful game rather than as a distasteful chore, the child will adopt your positive approach to these tasks.

You can also play sorting games at snack time. For example, you can place four different colored cups upside down on a table and hide a cracker under one of them (for example, the red one). Tell the child the cracker is under the red cup and see if she can find it. If she does not know where to look or if she picks up the wrong cup, reinforce her efforts and assist her. For example, you might say, "Ah, you picked up the blue cup and the cracker isn't there. Well, let's see, where is the red cup? There it is!" (Point to the red cup.) "Can you find the cracker under the red cup?" If the child picks up the red cup, positively reinforce her. If she hesitates, pick up the cup and let her get the cracker. Then try the game another day.

Art Games

PURPOSES: (1) To develop hand-eye coordination and manual dexterity and (2) to provide exploration of the sensory experiences stimulated by different textures, colors, sizes, and shapes.

MATERIALS: Crayons and a large sheet of paper.

ACTIVITY: Give the child a crayon and a large sheet of paper and watch what happens. If he does not discover how to mark on the paper, make a mark for him. The child may prefer playing with you instead of by himself. If so, you can make a mark on the paper, then let him make one, and continue taking turns. The child will imitate your actions, so make a

Fig. 5-20. By using your imagination, you can find many different ways for the child to draw.

variety of marks, such as horizontal, vertical, curvy or angular lines; dots; circles; triangles; and rectangles. Be creative! You may want to place paper over the entire surface that the child is marking on because he may not be able to confine his marks to the space provided by one sheet of paper.

You can progress to activities involving a wide variety of art materials. Some examples are as follows:

Pasting
Cutting with scissors
Finger painting
Body painting
Making objects out of clay
Wood working
Hammering
Different types of brush painting
Drawing with chalk
Making collages
Tearing
Making objects with papier mâché
Use your imagination. Almost anything that attracts the child's atten-

tion can be used as materials for these activities. Remember to emphasize the process, not the product. Encourage the child's exploration and positively reinforce his efforts.

Stacking Games

PURPOSES: (1) To develop hand-eye coordination, (2) to enable the child to relate the factors that affect balancing objects one on top of another, and (3) to explore and form associations between different shapes, sizes, textures, and colors.

MATERIALS: Commercial stacking toys, different sizes of tin cans, or small boxes. Paint some of the cans different colors or cover them with different colors of contact paper. (Be sure there are no sharp edges.) Cover the boxes or some of the cans with materials that have different textures, such as flannel, sandpaper, or furry material.

ACTIVITY: Give the child a group of similar objects such as blocks, cans, or small boxes. Encourage her to place these one on top of the other so they will balance. Combine the tasks of sorting and stacking by telling the child to stack up all the boxes or all the cans. Progress to having her stack all the objects that are the same color or all those that have a similar texture, such as all those that feel soft.

The Container and the Contained

PURPOSES: (1) To develop hand-eye coordination, (2) to form associations between objects that fit, and (3) to relate objects that are similar and recognize those that are different.

MATERIALS: Pots, pans, bowls, plastic food containers, plastic lids, different sizes of cans, small balls, and blocks.

ACTIVITY: Cut a round hole out of the center of a coffee can lid, just large enough for the balls to pass through. Have the child put the ball in the container through the round hole. Verbalize constantly and ask questions such as, "Where did the ball go?" The child will probably remove the lid and retrieve the ball.

When the child understands the idea of the game, add another challenge. Cut a square hole in the lid of a can, just large enough for the wooden blocks to pass through. Give the child the second can and the blocks, and let her practice putting the objects through the hole. Then give the child both cans and blocks. Watch to see if she associates the round objects with the round hole and the square objects with the square hole. You may need to practice this with the child or wait until she is a little older. Then you may want to add another shape such as a triangle to increase the challenge.

VARIATION: Another form of this game occurs when you use trays or boxes just large enough for the child's stacking objects to fit into. You can make cleanup chores fun-filled learning activities by providing containers that match the size, shape, or color of the play objects. Remember, however, that you must enthusiastically participate in the cleanup activities and verbalize concerning the characteristics of the objects being placed in the container and the way they fit into the spaces.

Retrieval Games

PURPOSES: (1) To enhance development of depth perception, (2) to provide practice in handling and controlling objects, and (3) to enable the child to recognize cause-and-effect relationships.

MATERIALS: A ruler, yardstick, wooden spoon, or similar implement.

ACTIVITY: A teachable situation occurs whenever any of the child's toys roll out of reach or under a piece of furniture such as a chair, sofa, or desk. Hand the child a stick or any other implement that will extend his reach. Encourage him to use the stick to reach the object and push it into a position where it can be retrieved. Provide reinforcement and assistance as needed to ensure the child's success.

You can vary the activity by suspending a yarn ball, balloon, or similar object just out of the child's reach overhead. Give the child a wooden spoon, ruler, or stick and encourage him to strike at the suspended object. Reinforce his efforts and when he hits the object, be especially enthusiastic.

Boogie Fever

PURPOSES: (1) To stimulate rhythmic responses, (2) to enhance language development.

MATERIALS: Records, record player, radio, or any type of musical instrument.

ACTIVITY: Young children readily respond to any kind of rhythmic stimulation. The ways you choose to stimulate rhythmic responses depend on your experiences and abilities. The most important thing is that you feel at ease in the situation. Remember, the child doesn't care about the quality of your voice, your ability to carry a tune or how rhythmic you are. Everyone can clap their hands, tap their feet, and sing children's songs. So just let go and enjoy yourself. If you need ideas, obtain some records and start humming, swinging, and move with the music. Most libraries have collections of records you can borrow. But if no other source is available, turn on the radio, or make your own music by beating on a pan with a wooden spoon. All you really need is the desire!

Sing to the child and invite her to sing along with you. Introduce finger play. An example of a song that is commonly used in this way is as follows:

> If you're happy and you know it,
> clap your hands (*repeat*)

If you're happy and you know it and you
    really want to show it,
If you're happy and you know it,
    clap your hands.

Repeat, substituting "stamp your feet," "shake your head," "swing your arms," and "clap your knees."

You need not limit yourself to songs other people have composed. The best rhythmic accompaniments are spontaneous expressions. So make up your own songs and create your own instruments. Something as simple as tapping out a rhythm with your hands, tapping two spoons together, or shaking your keys is as effective as anything else.

Toddlers enjoy dancing, and moving to a rhythmic beat is natural for them. So encourage their movement responses by playing stimulating music and by dancing with them. Don't be concerned about specific steps, just let go and move freely to the music.

Water Play

PURPOSES: (1) To enable the child to experience examples of concepts relative to volume and quantity, (2) to enable the child to see examples of cause and effect, (3) to enable the child to experience the sensory stimu-

Fig. 5-21. Squeezing water out of a plastic bottle enables the child to see "cause" and "effect."

lation of wetness and temperature change, and (4) to develop manipulative skills.

MATERIALS: Bathtub toys, bubble solution, plastic glasses, and a pitcher, bucket, or watering pot.

ACTIVITY: Young children enjoy water play, and developing a positive attitude toward the water is prerequisite to later water-safety training. Children should be given opportunities to enjoy water play in both indoor and outdoor environments. In some types of water play children can participate in a fairly independent manner, thereby developing the ability to be self-directing.

Indoor water play

Bathing should be a fun-filled activity. This means allowing time for the child to play in the water. You should chat with her about the temperature of the water, talk about what soap does, and verbalize as she washes her body parts. Provide sponges, plastic cups, and various floating objects. Show the child how these float when they are empty and sink when they are full of water. Bubbles are always fun. Ask the child to splash and stir the water to make bubbles with her hands, arms, the feet, and legs.

Children of this age also enjoy helping you wash the dishes. Be prepared for a little mess. However, the experience of helping is worth the extra effort. Just think how you feel when you think you are helping someone you love!

Children love to blow bubbles. Use a small pan with 2 to 3 inches of water in the bottom. Add a solution that will produce bubbles. (Be sure it is nontoxic.) Give the child a straw. Let her experiment by blowing in the straw and creating bubbles.

Pouring activities are excellent learning experiences. Provide the child with a pitcher and a couple of glasses. Put just enough water in the pitcher to almost fill one glass. This makes the pitcher lighter and also increases the child's success rate because she will probably try to pour all the liquid into the glass. The child may appear awkward at first, but as she continues to practice, she will become amazingly accurate. Because this activity tends to be messy, you may want to do it in the bathtub or outdoors.

Outdoor water play

A favorite outdoor water activity is sprinkler play. Children enjoy running in and out of the water, trying to catch it in a bucket, or just "sitting in the rain," feeling the water hit their bodies. A fun activity for children who are accustomed to being wet is the "on and off" game. While the child is playing in the sprinkler, turn the water off and tell the child "I'm turning the water off. There goes the water; it's all gone." The child's curiosity will draw him close to the sprinkler to see where the water went. Then tell the child, "I'm turning the water on. Here it comes." Children usually delight in the excitement this creates and will joyfully run from the spraying water.

Fig. 5-22. Children delight in the feeling and the effect of striking water with the hand.

You may find yourself repeating this game over and over because ordinarily children adore it.

Similar hose activities include letting the child fill buckets, water flowers, spray water on himself, and practice controlling the hose and the direction the water goes. Just let the child go and he will invent his own water games.

Summary

An infant is born unaware of herself and the world. This awareness gradually develops as the baby interacts with people and experiences the reality of objects, spaces, time, and cause and effect.

Language development parallels motor development and the two are inseparably interrelated. Movement activity serves as the learning medium for the child's physical development as well as for the development of concepts essential for language development.

For purposes of discussion, the phases of constructing the child's reality are designated as (1) the adjustment phase (birth to 1 month), (2) the sensory experiences phase (1 to 4 months), (3) the object experiences phase (4 to 8 months), (4) the space experiences phase (8 to 12 months), and the persistence phase (12 to 24 months). It is essential to provide varied and adequate stimulation to evoke the movement responses necessary for optimum development. The suggested activities accompanying the description of each developmental phase serve as guides to developing a program that will provide appropriate infant stimulation.

SUGGESTED READINGS

Braga, L., and Braga, J. *Children and adults: activities for growing together.* Englewood Cliffs, N.J.: Prentice-Hall, Inc., 1976.

Elkind, D. *The child's reality: three developmental themes.* New York: John Wiley & Sons, Inc., 1978.

Erikson, E. *Childhood and society* (2nd ed.). New York: W.W. Norton & Co., Inc., 1963.

Flavell, J.H. *The developmental psychology of Jean Piaget.* New York: D. Van Nostrand Co., 1963.

Gordon, I.J. *Baby learning through baby play: a parent's guide for the first two years.* New York: St. Martin's Press, Inc., 1970.

Lehane, S. *Help your baby learn—100 Piaget-based activities for the first two years of life.* Englewood Cliffs, N.J.: Prentice-Hall, Inc., 1976.

Levy, J. *The baby exercise book.* New York: Random House, Inc., 1977.

McDiarmid, N.J., Peterson, M.A., and Sutherland, J.R. *Loving and learning: interacting with your child birth to three.* New York: Harcourt Brace Jovanovich, Inc., 1975.

Piaget, J. *The construction of reality in the child.* New York: Basic Books, Inc., 1954.

Piaget, J. *Play, dreams and imitation.* New York: W.W. Norton & Co., Inc., 1962.

Piaget, J. *The child and reality: problems of genetic psychology.* New York: Penguin Books, 1976.

CHAPTER 6

Developing a movement vocabulary

A movement vocabulary is both verbal and nonverbal. The nonverbal component consists of body actions, and the verbal component consists of the words that describe how and where the body is moving. At first an infant's movement vocabulary comprises basic movements and the words that name these movements. For example, when learning to walk, an infant must also learn that the word *walk* is the name of that movement.

The infant's vocabulary develops while learning both movement and language skills. Thus by practicing new movement skills and by being taught the concepts that describe how and where she is moving, the infant's movement vocabulary becomes more extensive. In addition to the names of various movements, the child's vocabulary should be enlarged to include concepts relating to body awareness and spatial awareness (Table 1).

The key to developing a movement vocabulary is imitation. Therefore the primary role of the caregiver is that of a model. You must model both the movements and the verbalization. At first you can simply imitate the child's movements, then add the appropriate verbalization while encouraging the child to repeat your words. With older, more verbal infants, you can encourage them to verbalize their own actions. Finally you can move away from imitating and use only verbal suggestions. By observing the way children respond to your verbal prompting, you will be able to detect the areas in which they have mastered certain aspects of the movement vocabulary. You will also be able to note the situations in which you must continue the practice of imitation combined with verbalization.

Most children nearing the age of 2 years are able to begin progressing from activities that require only a physical response to activities that require them to respond both physically and verbally. An effective way to implement this change is through the use of imagery. Imagery is using a word that will evoke a mental image. For example, asking the child to move like a cat employs the mental image of a cat walking on all four feet. Because children love to imitate, using imagery is an effective teaching tool.

The activities we describe in this chapter were designed according to the Learning By Moving table on p. 100. You can create an endless variety of these kinds of learning activities by following the same procedure. It is really very simple once you become accustomed to working with the concepts listed in the table. Begin by observing the basic movement skills the

99

Table 1. Learning by moving

BASIC SKILLS	SKILLS BUILD CONCEPTS	BASIC CONCEPTS			
		Body awareness	**Spatial awareness**	**Spatial relationships**	**Time concepts**
Locomotor skills	Crawl Climb Walk Run Jump Gallop	Body parts Head Neck Shoulders Chest Trunk Arms Elbows Wrists Hands Fingers Legs Knees Ankles Feet Toes Back Hips Face Eyes Ears Nose Mouth Forehead	Direction Forward Backward Sideward Level High Low Size Big Little Shape Narrow Wide Path Straight Curved Angular	Up—down Inside—outside Near—far Over—under Around—through	Fast—slow Stop—go
Nonlocomotor skills	Bend and stretch Twist and turn Push and pull Swing and rock Fall and rise				
Manipulative skills	Toss Catch Kick Strike Swim				

child is able to execute. The skills young children typically evidence are listed in the basic skills section of the table. Select one or more of these skills, and use it as the medium for conceptual development. The concepts that children should learn by moving are listed under the headings "Body Awareness," "Spatial Awareness," "Spatial Relationships," and "Time Concepts." The second step in designing essential learning activities consists of referring to one of the concept categories and selecting the particular concepts you desire to introduce or reinforce.

Designing learning activities based on the Learning By Moving table consists of these three steps: (1) selecting the basic movement skill, (2) selecting the concepts, and (3) locating the objects or structures needed for the practice situation. We can use the Up and Down game on p. 104 to illustrate how learning activities are developed from the Learning By Moving table. Since this is a game for toddlers, we selected the skill of walking. Since walking is a locomotor movement, you know immediately that the child will be moving through space. So if you refer to the column under the heading "Spatial Relationships," you see "up—down" listed. You now have the skill of walking and the concepts of up and down. The next step is to look around and attempt to discover an appropriate learning environment for the activity. As suggested in the description of the Up and Down game, it may be necessary for you to construct some type of structure, or in some instances it may be possible to use natural features in the environment.

After the child has participated in the initial activity, you can extend it by adding other concepts. These will often emerge naturally as the child explores new movement possibilities. Variations of the Up and Down game are listed on p. 104. First we added the directional concepts of backward and sideward. Next we substituted body awareness concepts by referring to the body parts listed on the table and selecting body parts the child can walk on. In the third variation we emphasized the size of the steps, and in the fourth variation we introduced the time concepts of fast and slow.

Practicing the same skill over and over may cause the child to lose interest. If this happens, you can stimulate the child's interest by introducing a new skill that will review the same concepts. For example, you can substitute running or jumping as the skills used in the Up and Down game. You can also combine skills such as running up fast and walking down slow or walking up backward and running down forward.

As the child's movements become more skillful, you can design learning activities by selecting the body, spatial, or time concepts you want to reinforce and then selecting the particular skills that will serve as the learning medium. You can begin with any concepts on the table, but it is important that you remember to include all of the concepts eventually and to review them in different combinations. This will enable the child to recognize the concepts in different contexts.

The activities in this chapter are sequenced so that the child is first introduced to a variety of skills and to the words that describe these body actions. The activities are arranged so that they progress from simple to complex. This allows for a gradual increase in the skill level required and also in the complexity of thought and language required.

As the child participates in these activities also remember to give plenty of positive reinforcement. A child's movement patterns are correct for him at the time they are executed. Therefore he can *never* move incorrectly. Remember, too, that the child is learning how to learn, and an important aspect of this is to become success (not failure) oriented.

Locomotor skills

Walking, running, jumping, galloping, and climbing are locomotor skills. The term *locomotor* is used in reference to this group of skills because the body is moved through space from one place to another. It is normal for a child to be somewhat hesitant when first attempting these skills because each skill requires the child to coordinate movements in a unique way. This is why it is so important for caregivers to understand the demands each particular movement task places on the child.

WALKING

A new world opens up to the child as he begins to walk. The ability to maintain an upright body position and to move about freely gives the child a whole new perspective. The skill of walking may appear relatively simple, but it is actually quite demanding. Walking requires the maintenance of a balanced, upright body position while taking a step. Therefore two general movement abilities are essential: dynamic balance and strength.

The term *dynamic* refers to an individual moving through space; thus *dynamic balance* refers to an individual maintaining balance while moving. This is a much more complex task than maintaining balance while standing. That is why the infant falls down so often when he is learning to walk.

To walk, the child must have enough strength to maintain an upright body position. This means he is constantly resisting the force of gravity pulling his body downward.

The key to developing strength and dynamic balance is practice. The child should be stimulated to participate in tasks that gradually become more challenging. The length of time he practices should also be gradually increased.

Activities to develop walking skill
Back-and-Forth

A typical activity for the beginning toddler is the Back-and-Forth game. In this game two adults space themselves a short distance apart. The child walks back and forth between them as the adults say, "Walk," "Sally, walk," "Sally, walk to Daddy," or similar words.

When the child begins to assume an upright position and take her first steps, she may need your assistance. However, there are two things you should remember. One is that you should never hold the child's arms while assisting her. She needs to be able to move her arms freely to help maintain her balance. If you feel you must hold onto the child, hold her at the waist. It is better, however, to let her hold your arm. If the child is holding onto you, she can let go whenever she desires. Also you should never force the child or assist her in what she needs to do alone. For example, a toddler often loses her balance and falls. You should allow her to get up alone. You can position yourself so that she can use you to hang onto and to pull herself upright. But don't pick the child up! Getting up by herself helps her to develop strength and balance. If you are anxious and overly zealous, you will tend to inhibit the child's natural learning. Therefore while you work with toddlers, encourage, love, and reinforce them; but let the movement patterns emerge from the child. In this way the child will be a successful beginning walker and you will be a successful caregiver.

This game can be repeated over and over throughout the day as the child's interest permits. As her success rate increases, so should the distance between the adults. Increasing the distance provides more practice, and more practice builds additional strength and endurance.

Fig. 6-1. The ability to walk opens up a new and exciting world.

Here I Come

In the home or day-care center, the child will often attempt to walk from one place to another (such as from a chair to a sofa). To be sure that this will occur, you should plan for it. This is called the "Here I Come" game because the toddler seems to be thinking, "Look out, world; here I come."

Set up this game by estimating the distance your child usually walks before he resorts to crawling or some other means of locomotion. Devise a route for the child by placing stable objects at these resting places. These "rest areas" enable the child to stop and rest while maintaining a standing position. We use plastic cubes about 18 inches high, but anything that will not topple over when the child uses it for support can be used. The child must feel as though he is actually going someplace. Therefore you should place the rest areas in a path leading somewhere, such as from the living room to the kitchen or across the yard. To help the child make this association, stand at specific locations ahead of him and say, "Walk to me." This also places you in a position to reinforce the child's achievement.

Requiring the child to rely on objects rather than people for physical support is a step toward developing independence. It requires shifting from a dependence on the caregiver to dependence on objects that exist in the child's surroundings. This is an initial step for the child in learning to control himself within his world.

Up and Down

When walking has become the child's primary means of locomotion, he is ready to play the Up and Down game. In this game hills are used that exist in the natural environment. If you live where the land is flat, or if you are restricted to being indoors for long periods of time, ramps can be used. Introduce this game by using an incline with a 5-foot ramp rising to a height of 18 inches. Then vary the angles according to the child's skill level and his ability to complete the task. Walk up the ramp or hill; then walk back down while the child imitates your movements by following you. Be sure to verbalize about your actions. For example, as you walk say, "I am walking up and now I am walking down." This task involves several factors, and you must verbalize these for the child to make the association between his body position and the directions "up" and "down." Children usually enjoy this game because they find it challenging, and they will repeat it again and again. You must be patient and let them continue playing. When the child has mastered this skill, he will lose interest. When this occurs, introduce another activity or take a break. Remember, the key factors are *imitation* and *verbalization*.

The child will imitate both your actions and your words, although at first he may just say "up" or "down" and later "walk up" or "walk down." These responses may seem ordinary or unimportant to most adults. They are, however, an essential aspect of the toddler's developing ability to make the as-

Fig. 6-2. Walking up a ramp is easier than walking down.

sociations that increase his awareness of himself and the movement environment.

VARIATIONS:

1. Go up and down backward and then sideward.
2. Go up and down on different body parts, for example, on hands and knees or hands and feet.
3. Go up and down with big steps, then with little steps.
4. Go up and down faster and slower.
5. Walk up and roll down.

Remember to emphasize the language development aspect of these activities. Talk the child through each activity while encouraging him to repeat the words.

The various activities just described illustrate that walking is a very adaptable movement. Walking can be used to develop physical skills and abilities. In addition, it can be used as a means of introducing a number of concepts relative to the body and the way it moves through space.

Walking activities to develop body awareness

Continue using imitation and verbalization as you and the child participate in activities such as walking on the hands and feet, walking on the hands and knees, walking on the elbows and knees, or walking on one hand

Fig. 6-3. Walking with the hands up high is different than walking with the hands to the side.

and two feet. As you verbalize these actions, emphasize the name of the body action (walking) and the body parts being used. For example, you can say, "We are walking on our hands and knees," or "Now we are walking on our elbows and knees." You can try adding another dimension to these activities by using animal imagery. Name a familiar animal such as a dog, cat, or horse, and let the child pretend to be this animal while she is walking on her hands and feet or hands and knees. You can also add appropriate animal noises.

As children approach the age of 2 years, most of them are capable of mental representation in the form of visual coding. You can extend the use of this capability by showing the child pictures of various animals and challenging her to respond by making the appropriate noise, naming the animal, and walking like the animal.

In the activities just described, the child is required to relate only to her own body parts. The next step in the progression is requiring the child to associate similar activities by relating to another person's body parts.

Have another child or adult lie down on the floor, face up, with arms and legs extended sideward. Tell the toddler to follow you as you walk around the person lying on the floor. As you walk, step over various body parts, verbalizing the name of each part. For example, you could say, "I am stepping over Suzie's arm, over her leg, over her foot, and over her head." Next have the toddler lie down and, as you step over her body parts, verbalize their names. For example, you might say, "I am walking over your arm, over your hand, over your leg, and over your middle." Finally, lie down and let the child step over your body parts. At first let her go wherever she wants, while you verbalize the names of your body parts. Then see if you can verbalize first and have her follow your suggestions. For instance, you could say, "Can you walk over my arm? Can you walk over my knee? Can you walk over my head?" Finally, see if the child can verbalize correctly as she steps over the various parts of your body. Children usually enjoy a little rhythm and sequencing added to the game. You could lie down and rhythmically sing the words, "Over the arm, over the head, over the other arm, over the leg, over the other leg, over the middle, and sit—and I got you!" Now hug, laugh, and roll on the floor together until the child is ready to repeat the activity. Repetition is essential and is necessary to maintain the child's interest. So when you engage in activities with a child, be prepared to repeat them over and over again.

You will need an oversized drawing of a person for the following activities. You can use a large figure cut out of cardboard or a bed sheet. Commercial cardboard dolls are also available, especially around the holidays. Some examples are a big witch, a clown, or Santa Claus. However, you can also use colored chalk to draw a person on the driveway or sidewalk. Chalk washes off easily, and this provides another fun activity for the child.

The following progression illustrates how the body shape can be used:

1. Have the child imitate you as you walk to various body parts, stopping on each one and verbalizing the name of the specific part.

2. Have the child walk to various body parts as you verbalize what the child is doing. You can add variety by specifying a "home base" located several yards away from the body figure. Have the child walk from home base where you are standing to a specific body part and then walk back to you. When he returns to you, you can express your pleasure with loving attention.

3. Verbalize simple directions and see if the child can follow them. For example, say, "Walk to the head," "Walk to the eyes," or "Walk to the ears."

4. Link successive directions together. An example of such a sequence is to say, "Walk to the head, then to the foot." You may have to repeat the cues "head" and "foot" while the child is moving.

Fig. 6-4. Walking over and putting the fire hat on her friend "Sandy" involves body part recognition.

5. Have the child select different body parts, walk to each one, and verbalize each name.

The child's everyday walking activities also provide endless opportunities for the development of body awareness. As the toddler is walking toward you, you can say, "Jamie's feet are walking." If you want the child to come to you, instead of saying, "Come here," you can say, "Ask Ruby's feet to bring her here." Then when the child gets to you, you can review other body parts by saying

Put Sara's hands on my knees.

Put Tony's elbows on my hands.

Put Stacy's knees on my knees.

Put Lee's head on my knees.

Put Juliet's arms around my neck.

These instructions not only serve to review body parts concepts, but also provide additional ways for you and the child to touch each other and physically express affection.

Walking provides an endless array of learning possibilities. You and the child will be able to discover many others if you allow the child to explore freely. You must remember, however, to maximize the child's learning potential by encouraging verbalization of the names of body parts and body actions.

Walking activities to develop spatial awareness

Walking provides a medium in which the toddler can make the associations necessary to develop numerous spatial concepts. These concepts include

Direction	Forward, backward, sideward
Level	High, low
Size	Big, little
Shape	Wide, narrow
Pathway	Straight, curved, angular

When introducing concepts to young children, it is essential to remember that they cannot perceive gradual changes or slight differences. Therefore you must design practice situations involving contrasting concepts. This is illustrated in the list just given: forward is the opposite of backward; high is the opposite of low; and big is the opposite of little. When you introduce the child to spatial concepts, begin with the directional concepts. Concepts relating to direction are the easiest to learn because they are repeatedly moving in different directions during their ordinary daily activities.

Walking Forward and Backward

Activities emphasizing the direction in which the child is moving can be done anywhere. However, it is more convenient to use a hallway or some other narrow space when you introduce these concepts. This activity is similar to a "follow the leader" activity because the child imitates as you walk forward and backward. Of course, for the child to learn these concepts you must verbalize while you are moving. So you can say something like, "Here we go walking forward to the bathroom," or "Now we are walking backward to Jackie's room."

In our day-care center, we made the exploration of direction an outdoor activity by constructing a maze with several narrow passages just the right size for toddlers (Fig. 6-5). However, you can improvise a maze by using stakes driven into the ground with a rope tied between them. Using this type of rope structure is effective because the child can hold onto the rope while he is walking. This is not necessary for support, but it does encourage the child to walk backward because holding the rope prevents him from turning around.

Another forward-and-backward walking game that has proved stimulating involves the use of a child-size clothesline and a simple puzzle consisting of several pieces. First make a child-size clothesline using sticks and string. Then hang the puzzle pieces on the line with clothespins. Have the child walk forward and pick one of the pieces off the line. When he has all of the

Fig. 6-5. The pathways of a maze provide a learning medium for directional concepts.

pieces, assist him in putting the puzzle together. Repeat the activity, but challenge the child to walk backward to get the pieces. Remember that you are the model, so you must do the activity first and then let the child imitate.

If this activity is too simple or if the child needs variety, add another clothesline positioned so that the two are parallel. Have the child start at one line, walk forward to the second line, pick a puzzle piece, and then walk backward to the line where he started. Continue moving forward and backward in a zigzag fashion while the child imitates you until he has all the puzzle pieces. Remember to talk the child through the activity, emphasizing the directions in which he is moving.

Additional walking practice and concept learning can be stimulated by using lines or balance beams. Lines can be drawn with chalk on the sidewalk or made with masking tape. You can also use flour to make lines in the grass. First make two parallel lines about 8 to 10 inches apart. Have the child walk forward and then backward between the lines. You may want to increase the difficulty of the activity by making the two lines into a zigzagged or curved shape.

Balance beam activities are excellent. In addition to providing balance practice, they also require visual tracking. You should begin with a board 6 inches wide and 5 to 8 feet long. By using a board 6 inches wide, the child

Fig. 6-6. To step up onto a balance beam, a toddler must balance his body over the supporting foot.

can walk with both feet side by side. This gives the child a wider base of support than would be possible if the board were so narrow that he had to place one foot in front of the other.

Have the child walk forward and then backward on the beam while following you. Next you can raise the beam off the ground approximately 6 to 8 inches. This does not alter the skill, but it does add excitement. After the child becomes skilled in walking forward, you can use a beam that is 4 inches wide. This will require that the child place one foot in front of the other as he walks, thereby increasing the difficulty of the task. Finally you can raise the height of the 4-inch beam, but you should never raise it over 12 inches high. Remember, you should never create a task that will require you to assist the child, but you may allow him to hold onto you. As explained earlier, the reason is that you are nonverbally communicating to the child the extent of his ability to cope.

Walking Sideward

Walking sideward may seem to be a more difficult concept to get across to the child. However, this is largely dependent on the manner in which you introduce this concept. It will be easier if you introduce the activity in a narrow space where the only way the child can walk is sideward. You can design this type of space by using the wall as one plane and chairs as another plane, leaving only enough space for you and the child to squeeze through sideways. Remember, you must verbalize as you execute the movement.

Fig. 6-7. Toddlers enjoy the use of imagery by tiptoeing quietly as they sneak up on the "sleeping giant."

When you feel the child understands the concept of sideways, add it to the forward-and-backward walking activities previously described. This will enable the child to recognize the differences between these three directions.

The child will learn more easily if you verbalize directions whenever the opportunity arises. For example, you can point out that the car is going forward or backward or that the grocery cart is moving forward or backward. You can also reinforce these concepts by pointing out how bugs, birds, or other animals move.

Walking on High and Low Levels

Introducing the concepts of *high* and *low* makes possible the creation of many new activities. It also opens the way for you to introduce the concepts of *over* and *under*.

Begin by walking on tiptoe. You may want to raise your arms high over your head to emphasize the idea of being up high. Next you can bend your knees so that you are walking on a low level. It is not necessary to make these activities exciting because the challenge of the skill creates enough excitement for the toddler. Have the child imitate walking on tiptoe while you emphasize the verbal association. Then introduce walking low. As the child approaches the age of 2 years, she may evidence an interest in pretending. In this case you can use imagery by "walking high like a giraffe" or "walking low like a duck." You can also use pictures portraying high and low movements. The world is filled with examples of high and low levels; by being alert to these examples, you can create numerous learning situations. Examples might be birds flying high or a bug crawling low. You may want to have the child change from walking to crawling to emphasize the difference between walking high and crawling low.

Walking with Big and Little Steps

The concept of *size* can be effectively introduced by simply having the child imitate you. You can take big steps while saying, "Look at my big steps," and then have the child imitate you. Next take some steps while saying, "Look at my little steps."

Examples of the concepts of *big* and *little* occur frequently in the child's everyday world, and his learning can be extended by calling attention to these instances. For example, you can say, "See my big shoes and your little shoes," or "See the big bus and the little car." You can determine whether or not the child has formed the associations necessary to distinguish these differences by placing a large cup and a small one side by side on the table. Then ask the child to take the big cup and see if he responds correctly.

Walking with Wide and Narrow Steps

Walk, taking steps with your feet wide apart while saying, "Look at my wide steps." Let the child walk between your legs while you are standing with your feet wide apart. You can have the child stand with her feet apart

Fig. 6-8. From walking with the feet wide apart, the child can progress to rocking from side to side.

while you roll a ball or some other toy back and forth between her legs. You can walk around the room or the yard, taking wide steps as you chase the child, and then walk over her when you catch up. Later this activity can develop into a game such as "Here Comes the Giant." This is similar to the activity we have just described, in that you chase the child. However, it becomes a game by adding the element of imagery. Stimulating the child's imagination with the image of you being a "giant" chasing her makes the activity different, thereby adding variety.

Toddlers tend to walk with their feet rather far apart, so the concept of *narrow* is more difficult for them to apply. You can change the position of your feet from wide apart to close together, and point out to the child that she can't get through when the space is narrow. You can then have the child put her feet close together while you attempt to put a toy between them, pointing out that it won't fit.

The concept of narrow can also be emphasized by having the child walk through narrow spaces as you describe how she must squeeze through.

Walking Along a Pathway

A pathway is simply a marked path (the space between two lines). This concept can be introduced anytime the toddler is moving in an area marked in some manner. You simply say, "Now we are walking along a path." (The use of the word "path" rather than "pathway" is preferable because it is a shorter word and means the same thing.) The child will be able to perceive the concept more clearly if you work with contrasting pathways. Therefore you should move along straight, curved, and angular paths. You can devise an infinite variety of different paths by using string, rope, tape, or paint on a hard surface. And you can locate paths in the environment (such as sidewalks) or devise paths by laying a string or other marker beside a piece of furniture such as a sofa. Be creative! Remember, your goal is to enable the child to practice walking and at the same time to perceive the concept of following a path.

RUNNING

As soon as the toddler feels confident while walking, she will naturally progress to running. In her first attempts she may just walk quickly; then with daily practice a running pattern begins to emerge. Just as we used the basic skill of walking to introduce body and spatial awareness concepts, we use the skill of running to review these concepts and to introduce others necessary to know for the child to form associations.

We have recently witnessed the advent of the jogging craze among adults. This indicates a trend toward people becoming more concerned about their health and sets an excellent example for children. You can use this activity as a learning situation by pointing out the runners to your child and verbalizing the action by saying something like, "See the woman running." Then you can ask, "What is the woman doing?" and wait for the child's response.

Once the child begins running, she will frequently use the skill in place of walking. You should encourage the child to attempt to run as soon as you detect that her walking pattern is a stable and efficient skill. Do this by using imitation and by verbally encouraging the child to "go fast." In your verbalizations it is helpful if you begin by saying, "Let's go fast, faster, faster." Then each time you say "faster," increase the speed of your voice and raise the pitch to accompany a more rapid movement.

Running is a very versatile activity that offers a wide variety of readily available learning opportunities. For example, you could develop the habit of running everyday with the child. This will increase your endurance as well as hers and will help develop her leg strength. "Chase" is a fun game because both of you can run while taking turns chasing and catching each other and then have a loving interaction afterward. As the child becomes more confident, you can make the chase game more difficult by changing directions rapidly when you are just out of reach of the child. This requires the child to change directions quickly, thereby providing the practice necessary to develop agility.

Because the young child tires easily, you must limit her to running short distances, such as across the yard and back. However, you should gradually

Fig. 6-9. These toddlers evidence different developmental stages of the skill of running.

increase the amount of her running practice by challenging her to participate in activities requiring her to run more often and to run a little farther and a little faster. By gradually increasing the demands of the task, you are constantly challenging the child and at the same time providing the kind of practice that will develop the general movement abilities of strength, balance, and coordination. This goal can be achieved by:

1. Increasing the number of times the child runs each day
2. Encouraging the child to run increasingly greater distances
3. Using inclines or hills that will cause the child to run up and down slopes

The following activities can be used to review body and spatial awareness concepts while providing practice situations aimed at achieving these three goals of strength, balance, and coordination:

Run forward.
Run backward.
Run sideways. (This is difficult for young children.)
Run up high.
Run down low.
Run with little steps.
Run with big steps.
Run straight.
Run in circles.
Run on hands and feet.
Run on hands and knees.

Remember to use modeling behavior and verbalization to encourage the child's participation and enhance her learning. The child may experience difficulty when attempting some of these activities. However, she does need to be challenged so if you think she is ready, go ahead and introduce them, remembering to reinforce all attempts and to encourage exploration.

Activities to develop time concepts

Children need to be specifically introduced to the concepts of *fast* and *slow*. You cannot assume that they will learn to recognize these concepts purely by chance. Running is an excellent skill to use in teaching these concepts because when you run you move fast.

Begin by having the child imitate as you run fast and then slow. (Children will usually walk when you say slow because they are unable to maintain their balance while running slowly.) By doing this activity, the child will naturally begin to associate the words "run" with fast and "walk" with slow. In these activities you should use the progression participate-model. That is, participate with the child and use verbal cues and questions as described on p. 40. It is essential to question the child because it assists her in language acquisition and at the same time reinforces forming associations. In this progression your questions should resemble the following with your selection depending on the child's cognitive level.

Question	Response
Are you running fast?	Yes
Are you running fast or slow?	Fast
What are you doing?	Running fast

At the same time you are working with the concepts of fast and slow, you can introduce the concepts of *stop* and *go*.

As always, begin by using imitation. First you can simply demonstrate that when you say "go" you run, and when you say "stop" you quit running. Start whenever the child is ready by saying, "Let's go!" Then while you are both running say, "Let's stop." Reward the child for stopping. This is a difficult skill to learn because it involves a great deal of body control. You must

Fig. 6-10. When children learn the meaning of the word "stop," they can associate it with signals (such as an upraised hand), signs, and colors.

make stopping into a fun activity because the child already knows running is fun and she won't want to stop. Stop-and-go activities can be used with any skill and with combinations of body and spatial concepts. For example, you might say, "Let's run up close to the fence. Go; stop." Or you might say, "Let's run on our hands and feet. Go; stop."

Activities combining walking, running, and crawling

As the child acquires new skills, you need to emphasize activities that will enable her to detect differences between the skills. For instance while the child is running, you can play the walk-run differentiation game. In this game you call out to the child to "walk" with you, and the child responds by walking; then you call out "run" and you both run. Vary the speed in which you make the calls. This enhances the skill of listening and develops the child's ability to move and to listen at the same time. The ability to move and to listen at the same time is an essential skill for young children to acquire because their world revolves around their moving body.

Once the child is able to repeatedly imitate the walk-run differentiation game, you can add the skill of crawling. When you feel the child is confident, you can stop participating as a model and just provide verbal cues, such as calling out different directions. Then you observe as the child displays her knowledge, repeating activities and acting as a model whenever necessary. Continue to vary the spatial and body awareness concepts used in the game. The following list exemplifies the progression you can use as you add concepts:

Walk backward.
Run forward.
Walk on your hands and feet.
Run on your hands and feet.
Walk with little steps.
Run with little steps.
Walk with big steps.
Run with big steps.
Walk in circles.
Run in circles.

Remember, when you first introduce a skill or concept, participate as a model and then progress to using only verbal stimulation.

Activities combining spatial concepts

As the child repeatedly experiences the application of spatial concepts, it is necessary to combine different dimensions so that he can make additional associations between movement and space. The exact time when this should occur depends on the child's readiness. Begin combining concepts when the child has shown that he "knows" the concepts separately. The readiness for combinations usually emerges at about the same time as the ability to run.

Following are examples of combinations you can use as a guide. These may be used with either walking or running, but in these examples we refer to running. While you participate as a model, encourage the child to attempt the following:

Run forward as low as you can be.
Run forward as high as you can be.
Run backward with little steps.
Run backward with big steps.
Run sideward with wide steps.

At first you should combine only two dimensions as illustrated by these examples. Then when these combinations no longer appear to be challenging, progress to combining three concepts. Following are examples of three dimensions:

Run forward in a circle using big steps.
Run backward along a line using little steps.
Run forward in a circle while being as high as you can.
Run forward in a circle using your hands and feet.

Most children at this age will not be able to combine more than three dimensions. Remember, the goal is not *how many* dimensions can be combined, but the development of the cognitive associations that make the child aware of how he *can* combine these dimensions.

Activities to develop spatial relationships

Spatial relationships may be defined as the way we can spatially relate our bodies to objects and structures. Common spatial relationships are as follows:

Inside—outside
Under—over
Near—far
Around—through

This list illustrates that these are pairs of opposites. Pairing these concepts when introducing them to the child enables him to differentiate between them because they are contrasting concepts.

You should begin with the spatial relationships that you and the child experience most often. In most instances, examples of these relationships will be found *inside* or *outside* your house during your daily routines. Examples may also be found anytime you enter or leave a room in the house.

We have found that the most efficient way to develop the child's knowledge of spatial relationships is by using "play objects." For this activity in our day-care center we use a 36 × 36 × 36 inch wooden box with two ends open, a ramp on the closed side, and stairs on the other side (Fig. 6-11). The box is large because to use modeling first an adult must be able to easily fit under the ramps and through the box. Once the child has made the association and no longer needs a model, child-size play objects can be used. The activity consists of you as the participant-model running inside the box and verbalizing your actions by saying, "I am running inside the box." After the child has followed you inside, you say, "Now we are inside." Then you say, "Here I go running outside the box." You then stop and say, "Now I am outside," as the child follows. Next have the child run inside and outside alone. If you think the child's verbal skills are adequate, ask questions while he is inside or outside. For example, when the child gets inside the box ask

Question	Response
Are you inside?	No or Yes
Are you inside or outside?	Inside
Where are you?	Inside *or* Inside box

The difficulty level of the question you ask depends on the child. The third question is more difficult than the first question. Therefore you would begin with the first question and progress to the third question when repeating the activity. You can then repeat this activity, substituting the spatial relationships of over and under, around and through, and near and far.

Children must make the association that spatial relationships apply to people as well as to objects. In the following activity you will need to demonstrate with an older child or another adult. Have the person assist you by forming a body shape you can go under. For example, have the person make a bridge by supporting himself on his hands and feet or hands and knees. Any shape is fine as long as you can crawl under it. Verbalize as you go under the person's body. Then have the child follow you as you go under.

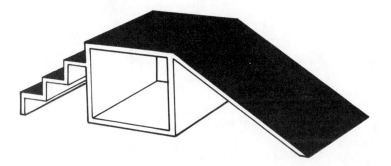

Fig. 6-11. Play objects that permit adult participation encourage modeling and interaction activities.

Fig. 6-12. Asking questions while children play encourages them to express in words what their bodies are doing. This young toddler replied, "Getting out."

Fig. 6-13. Adults and children can use their bodies as play objects.

Next you can make a shape and have the child run or walk under you. Finally you can have the child make a shape and you can try to go under him. You won't fit, of course, so you can discuss the fact that you are "too big." Emphasize the concept "big" as you both playfully tumble down. Repeat this activity substituting the spatial relationships of over, around, through, near, and far.

JUMPING

At the same time the child is practicing walking and running, she is also developing the movement abilities of strength, balance, coordination, and agility. These abilities are prerequisite to jumping because this skill involves taking off from one or both feet, being momentarily suspended in midair, and landing on both feet. Therefore to execute a jumping pattern, the child must have developed sufficient leg strength to initiate an upward thrust against gravity and enough balance to orient herself both in the air and when landing.

Children can be introduced to jumping as soon as they have developed a basic walking pattern. It will take time and a great deal of practice for the child to develop a skilled jumping pattern. To introduce this skill, simply jump up and down on the floor and see if the child will imitate you. At first

Fig. 6-14. Jumping (the ability to become airborne) is an exciting developmental skill.

you will probably notice that the child bounces without her feet moving. This is a good beginning because the child thinks she is jumping and is having fun doing it. Next the child may pick up one foot while the other foot remains firmly placed on the floor. This indicates that the child has become aware that something needs to leave the floor. You and the child should practice jumping in this manner everyday. Practicing in this way helps to develop leg strength and balance.

In addition to taking off from the floor, the child should begin jumping down from something. Jumping down requires less strength because the force of gravity is *assisting* rather than *resisting* the movement. The child's first downward movement will usually be to step down from a stair step or a stool. After this the child will progress to jumping down from a low, stable

Fig. 6-15. The skill of jumping downward often emerges as an exaggerated step.

object. Always let your child hold onto you for assistance if she desires, but never hold onto the child unless absolutely necessary for safety reasons. When you demonstrate jumping, exaggerate the bending of the knees and the two-foot takeoff. If you provide play objects of various heights for the child to jump down from and encourage daily practice, the child will quickly become more skilled.

As the child becomes more skilled at jumping down, he will also become more skilled at jumping up. Daily practice combined with encouragement and reinforcement is the key to skill improvement. The child should always be encouraged to try, but *never* forced to participate. If you are enthusiastic and provide opportunities for fun-filled daily practice, the child approaching 2 years of age will soon be a successful jumper. It will not be a mature,

Fig. 6-16. Jumping downward into a hoop can be followed by jumping inside and outside of it.

coordinated jump, but the child will be able to conquer gravity by leaving the ground with two feet and then landing on two feet in a balanced position.

Once the child has learned to execute a basic jumping pattern, you should begin assisting him in making concept associations. Begin by introducing the spatial dimensions separately. For example

Jump forward.
Jump backward.
Jump sideways.
Jump up.
Jump down.
Jump real big.
Jump real small.
Jump with legs wide apart.
Jump with legs together.
Jump straight ahead.
Jump in circles.

These skills require constant practice. The child may be completely successful or only partially successful. The primary goals are that the child attempts the skill and makes concept associations rather than that the child develops skills. Remember, the child is learning how to learn as well as learning specific skills and concepts.

Because jumping down is an easier skill than jumping up, begin association activities by having the child jump down. Provide a play object for the child to jump down into, such as a hoop or a rope in the shape of a circle. The child can jump inside the circle or jump outside the circle. Raise the hoop off the ground about 6 to 8 inches, and have the child jump down from a low object and into the hoop.

Jumping up will be the next skill. Use a play object such as a hoop or a rope and have the child jump over, jump around, jump through, jump inside, and jump outside the object.

You can substitute jumping for walking and repeat the activities de-

Fig. 6-17. A bounding board provides excellent jumping practice.

scribed on p. 107. The child jumps over various parts of your body and verbalizes each of them. This could be hazardous to you, so use your own judgment. If you feel nervous and scared or if you doubt your child's ability to successfully jump over parts of your body, *don't* do the activity. Your nonverbal language will tell the child, "I don't think you can do it." You can do the same activity using a body shape made out of cardboard (see Figs. 5-18 and 7-6).

Make various shapes with your body and have the child jump off different body parts. Ways to do this are as follows:

Lie face down on the floor or position yourself on your hands and knees. Have the child climb up and jump down off your back.

Position yourself face up on your hands and feet in a crab walk position and have the child jump off your knees, abdomen, or chest.

Additional activities can be created by making various shapes and having the child jump under you, through you, in a straight line, or in circles as he goes under the bridge formed by your body. You could also have the child jump fast, hard, soft, close to you, or far away from you.

GALLOPING

Galloping is a combination of walking and running, with the same foot leading continuously. This is the first locomotor skill to appear in the developmental sequence that is actually a combination of two basic skills. The child will later develop two other locomotor skills that combine two basic skills. These will be skipping and sliding.

Galloping is reported in almost all of the literature as an advanced skill, usually emerging when children are 4 to 6 years old. However, in a sample of 200 children, we have seen at least 80 percent of them gallop before the age of 2 years. This fact clearly evidences a discrepancy between children's capabilities and the motor development literature. This may occur because children learn by imitation. Therefore if they have not been introduced to the skill of galloping, the association between the two prerequisite skills cannot be made and the skill will not emerge, even though the readiness for it has developed. This reemphasizes the fact that for associations to be made, the concepts must be introduced and the child must participate in practice situations that provide opportunities for the associative factors to occur. Furthermore, the child must be reinforced. When these conditions are not present, the forming of associations is left to chance, thereby being delayed or failing to occur.

Children should be introduced to the skill of galloping as soon as they can walk and run fairly well. Introduce the skill through participant-modeling and verbalization of the actions. Using imagery is an effective way of practicing galloping because it is the locomotor movement associated with horses. So you can have the child ride a stick horse or gallop like a pony. You can effectively use galloping to provide practice situations for body and spa-

Fig. 6-18. Children learn by imitating other children as well as adults.

tial awareness concepts. For example, the child can be a pony who is galloping over, under, around, into, through, or out of objects and spaces.

CLIMBING

Climbing is an extension of crawling; therefore many infants can climb up steps before they can walk. The movement patterns of climbing are similar to crawling except that young children usually lead with one side of the body. At first infants will typically descend by coming down head first. Some experimenting is required for them to discover that it is best to descend backward.

As soon as a child has learned to walk, he will usually attempt to climb up and down steps in an upright position, *marking time* on each step. Mark-

Fig. 6-19. By climbing up and down, children learn about themselves and about their environment.

ing time means that he goes up one step at a time, placing both feet on each step, and then leads with the same foot each time he takes the next step.

Children need extensive climbing practice. Climbing activities contribute to the development of strength, balance, and coordination. To develop these general movement abilities, children must have opportunities to (1) increase the number of steps or rungs to climb, (2) increase the number of times they climb up and down the steps or ladder, and (3) increase the difficulty of the climbing activity.

To provide an opportunity for the child to increase the number of steps or rungs he climbs, you will need ladders or staircases with different numbers of steps. Many modern homes do not have staircases. If these are not available in the home or day-care center, freestanding steps can be made or purchased. However, if you look around your neighborhood or throughout your community, you can locate a variety of steps. Traveling to these locations serves two purposes. It provides novel and varied practice situations and serves as a fun-filled field trip.

Some commercial manufacturers design steps consisting of three steps up and three steps down and ladders with three rungs. There is nothing standard about the number 3. Any number of steps will do as long as they are scaled to the child's size and are a safe height. Variety is an important factor because this is what stimulates interest.

Increasing the number of times a child climbs up and down the steps or ladder requires a great deal of patience on your part. Children love to climb. Most children will climb until they are exhausted and, as a result, they may fall. You must be aware of this possibility and, when the child seems tired, move on to an activity that requires use of different muscle groups. On the other hand, if the child becomes bored easily, you can do a number of things to stimulate participation. You can offer encouragement, provide a variety of climbing apparatus, or introduce body and spatial concepts.

The way a person gives encouragement is an expression of individuality. However, we suggest using both physical and verbal encouragement. An example of physical encouragement is to stand at the top or bottom of the climbing structure, and when the child arrives, welcome her with hugs and kisses. A word of caution, however. Too much encouragement can cause an accident. The child may get so excited that she is unable to pay attention to what she is doing and thus may become totally goal oriented rather than task oriented. You will have to be a sensitive observer to detect the difference between the two.

The second suggestion is to offer a variety of climbing apparatus. This will be discussed in detail in Chapter 7, which deals with designing learning environments. Providing a variety of climbing equipment for a young child is really quite simple. Young children have static perceptions of reality. In the mind of the young child, a ladder leaning against the house differs from the same ladder laying on the ground. Therefore you can use the same equipment and add "newness" by changing its position, its function, and its relationship to other objects. We also suggest that you introduce body and spatial concepts to encourage the child to practice. These activities have been described in the sections dealing with walking, running, and jumping.

For the child to develop climbing ability, it is important to increase the difficulty of the activity. In other words, offer a progression from simple to complex. The following principles explain why some climbing activities are more difficult than others. This information will assist you in devising an appropriate progression for each child.

1. *It is easier to go up steps than it is to go down steps.* When going up, the child moves forward in the direction she is looking, but when moving down, she is going backward.

Fig. 6-20. Various climbing structures are manufactured commercially.

For slightly older children, it is still easier to go up rather than down the steps, but for a different reason. The older child will turn around so that she moves in a forward direction while going down as well as while going up. But going down the steps requires that the child balance herself on one supporting leg that is bent during the time the stepping leg reaches downward to the next step.

2. *It is easier to climb up a ladder than down a ladder.* This is true because climbing up a ladder involves a hand-hand-foot-foot sequence with the initial movements of hand-hand directly in the visual field. Climbing down requires a foot-foot-hand-hand sequence; during this sequence the line of vision is blocked by the body.

3. *It is easier to climb both steps and ladders when the distance separat-*

ing the steps or rungs is small. If the steps are large, more leg strength is required for the child to overcome the force of gravity and lift her body the additional distance. Also since the distance is greater, the child must support herself on a small base of support for a longer period of time.

4. *The smaller the angle of incline of the ladder, the more difficult the climbing skill. For example, a ladder leaning against the house at a 60-degree angle is easier to climb than a ladder at a 30-degree angle.* A ladder with a larger angle of incline is easier to climb because the child's body is in a more upright position. In an upright body position, the child's head is above her base of support, making it easier to balance. A smaller angle puts the child's body in a position where her head is over the base of support. Thus additional strength and balance are required to maintain this unstable body position. This factor is an important consideration because of the size and weight of the young child's head in relation to the rest of her body.

Fig. 6-21. The ladder's angle of incline has an effect on the difficulty of the skill.

5. *The smaller the base of support, the more difficult the skill.* This principle explains why ladders with circular rungs are more difficult to climb than ladders with flat rungs.

6. *The less stable the base of support, the more difficult the skill.* Wooden or aluminum ladders are easier to climb than rope ladders with rungs that "give" when weight is applied.

Climbing is an essential locomotor activity in which young children can safely participate. This is an important concept for parents and caregivers to understand. If the adult perceives an activity as dangerous and displays even the slightest amount of reluctance because of fear, this attitude is passed on directly to the child who then becomes afraid. Transference of this fear is unfair to the child because it is not founded in fact and thus is detrimental to healthy development.

If you look at climbing as another potentially fun-filled activity that benefits your child and if you follow the safety guidelines described below, your child will be able to enjoy participating in these essential activities.

1. At appropriate times and under safe conditions let the child fail and fall. This will enable him to come to know his own limitations. Remember to encourage him to keep trying.

2. When assisting a child who is climbing a ladder, loosely hold onto his ankles and assist only when necessary. Let the child strain and struggle.

3. When supervising the child, concentrate on his feet. The child can see where to place his hands, but the feet are not directly in line with the child's vision.

4. Teach your child to hang from the ladder. This will enable the child to make the association, "If I hold on, I do not fall." If you see the child beginning to slip, emphasize holding on by cupping your hand over his hand and the rung. Let the fall continue, but remind the child to hold on so he will not fall the next time.

5. Do not allow the child to hold any objects in his hands while climbing. Children like to hold tiny objects in their hands, but this can be dangerous while climbing. Sometimes small objects are hard to spot, so check the hands of the child before beginning climbing activities.

Activities to develop climbing skill

Prewalking children need to practice climbing up steps on all fours (hands and feet). Not only will the change in level provided by the steps present climbing opportunities, but it also assists the young child in assuming an upright body position.

If the child is hesitant, encourage him to climb. Enable the child to practice alone as well as with you. As you and the child practice climbing together, you should imitate his actions. In this way, a simple and rewarding

Fig. 6-22. As infants become mobile, they need opportunities to climb.

up-and-down climbing activity will evolve. This procedure develops as follows:

The child climbs up the steps.

You climb up the steps the same way the child did.

The child climbs down the steps.

You climb down.

As time goes on, you may begin climbing up and down together. You may position yourself on all fours on top of the child and climb in this manner. For safety reasons be careful not to obstruct the child's vision. Verbalize your actions for the child. For example

I am climbing up the steps on my hands and knees.

I am climbing down the steps on my hands and knees.

We are climbing together.

I am climbing up the steps behind you.

As the child becomes capable of upright locomotion (walking), climbing becomes more refined and additional practice is necessary. Therefore you should take advantage of every opportunity that occurs in daily life. For example, you could practice while going into a store or getting out of the car. Be patient and let the child climb up and down the best way she can. Try not to put yourself in a situation where you must hurry and pick up the

Fig. 6-23. Hanging from a ladder requires confidence in yourself.

child to save time. Real-life activities present the best practice situations, so be alert to using them to enhance the child's development.

If a child needs assistance while attempting to climb steps, encourage her to use a rail if one is available. If a rail is not available, let the child hold onto you. Never hold onto the child because this restricts her and often means that you are doing the activity *for* her.

After the child has had some stair-climbing experience, introduce him to climbing a ladder. Some common ladder activities are as follows:

Climbing up the ladder

Climbing down the ladder

Climbing up or down to a specified rung and sitting on the ladder

Hanging from the ladder

Dropping from a hanging position
Sitting on a rung and lowering the body through the rungs to a hanging
position

Activities to develop body and spatial concepts while climbing

When the child has developed some confidence in her ability, you can
progress to using climbing as a means of reviewing body and spatial concepts.

Put your hands on the ladder.*
Put your foot on the ladder.
Put both feet on the ladder.
Put your head on the ladder.
Put your chin (elbow[s], knee[s]) on the ladder.

It is best to have the child stand on the ground when you begin associating body parts with the ladder. Then you can progress to having the child
stand on a lower rung and repeat the body part activities. If the child is
ready for an even greater challenge, have her climb with different body
parts. For example, she could climb with her hands and knees or with one
hand and both knees. This is fairly difficult, but if your child is ready don't
limit her experimentation or hamper her curiosity.

You can introduce the concepts of *stop, fast,* and *slow* to the child by
having him

Climb up the ladder, stop, and sit on a rung.
Climb up the ladder, stop, and hang.
Climb up the ladder fast and climb down the ladder slow.

Climbing is an excellent activity in which to review spatial concepts. The
following activities evidence this learning potential.

Have the child climb up as high as he desires, and give him time at the
top to be "tall." Point out things in the environment such as trees, the road,
other people, or anything else the child might enjoy seeing from his "new"
perspective. Have the child climb down and be "low"; then have the child
climb up forward and down backward. As the child becomes more adept at
climbing, he may want to climb down in a forward position. If the rungs of
the ladder are not too far apart, have the child climb with big steps (skipping
a rung), climb with his feet or hands wide apart, or climb with his feet or
hands close together. Use the ladder in combination with other equipment
and have the child

Climb up the ladder and inside a box.
Climb down the ladder and outside a box.
Climb up the ladder and through a tunnel.
Climb up the ladder and over a box.

---

*Since these instructions are addressed to the child, the word *ladder* is used in place of the
word *rung*.

Fig. 6-24. Rope ladders provide excellent climbing practice.

You can also combine climbing with various locomotor and nonlocomotor skills to create challenging learning activities. Examples of these kinds of combinations are as follows:

Climb up the ladder, onto a box, and jump off.

Climb up the ladder and slide down a slide.

Climb down the ladder, stop, turn, and jump off the rung.

Hang from the ladder and swing.

Hang from the ladder and bend.

Run under the ladder and then climb up it.

Climb up the ladder and down the stairs.

Pull the ladder over to a beam.

Lay the ladder on the ground and walk through the spaces.

Lay the ladder on the ground and walk on the rungs.

Repeat these activities while going backward and sideward.

Once the child has experience with steps and hard-runged ladders, progress to using a rope ladder. This increases the skill requirement and presents a new challenge to the child. You can repeat all the previous activities using the rope ladder. Rope ladders also offer the opportunity to combine manipulative skills. This does not mean that manipulative skills cannot be combined with stair steps (such as kicking the ball off the steps, or tossing the ball up the steps and catching it) or hard-runged ladders, but that a rope ladder is more versatile and we have found it to be safer. We made our rope ladder from an old swing set (Fig. 6-24). The rope rungs are 8 inches apart,

Fig. 6-25. Hanging from a rope ladder allows a child to view the world from upside down.

which has proved very suitable. In addition to the activities previously mentioned, we developed the following:

Hanging upside down

Sitting and swaying

Sitting and bouncing

Standing and bouncing

Crawling through the rungs

Placing a ramp on the rope ladder and running up the ramp, climbing the ladder, and running back down the ramp

Tossing a large ball up on the ropes and trying to catch it as it works its way down

Placing a large ball between the ropes and striking it with different body parts, causing it to pop out the other side

Placing a large ball between the rope rungs, then hanging and swinging to kick the ball with the feet

Continue to use both your imagination and the child's imagination to create novel climbing activities. Remember that being "up at the top" of objects and structures affords the small child the opportunity of viewing the world from an adult perspective and that this is an exciting experience!

Nonlocomotor skills

The skills of crawling, climbing, walking, running, jumping, and galloping are locomotor movements. They are called locomotor skills because they are used to move one's body through space from one place to another. The development of these skills parallels the development of companion skills that we call nonlocomotor movements. The term *nonlocomotor* refers to a group of skills that includes bending and stretching, pushing and pulling, twisting and turning, swinging and rocking, and falling and rising.

Infants begin executing bending, stretching, and twisting movements as soon as they are born. Very soon they begin pulling with their hands and pushing with their hands and feet. All these movements are essential for the development of the strength and coordination necessary in the execution of more complex skills. As soon as the baby develops sufficient strength, he will turn (roll) over. Development of the ability to sit upright in a balanced position frees the arms to swing and the upper body to rock. When the child begins to stand and walk, falling and rising become common movement patterns. Falling down and struggling to get back up serve as important functions in learning. The child is learning how to balance and at the same time is developing arm and leg strength.

Infants learn to execute nonlocomotor skills before they are developmentally ready to learn the accompanying language skills. For this reason it is easy for adults to overlook the importance of the child's verbal learning. However, if you neglect this aspect of the child's early learning, he will simply go through the motions of executing physical skills without paying attention to the actions or understanding their effects. This is similar to reading words and not understanding the meaning behind them. However, our goal is for children to master both skill execution and understanding. This means that while the child is refining these skills, he is also learning how to identify them and how to form associations.

Because the child does not need to move from one place to another to execute nonlocomotor movements, you can easily incorporate practice of these movements into daily routines such as eating, diaper changing, and bathing. You can broaden the child's learning experiences by assisting her in making the association that one can execute nonlocomotor movements while standing, sitting, or lying down. Adults often assume that if the child bends and stretches while standing, she will know she can also do it while sitting. We cannot assume the child will transfer this information from one situation to another. We must assist the child to make these associations by having her execute the skill while her body is in different positions. Then while she is participating in the activity, you can point out that she is doing the same skill. For example, you could have the child bend and stretch her arms while sitting, then have her bend and stretch her arms while standing up.

The fact that nonlocomotor movements can be performed while children

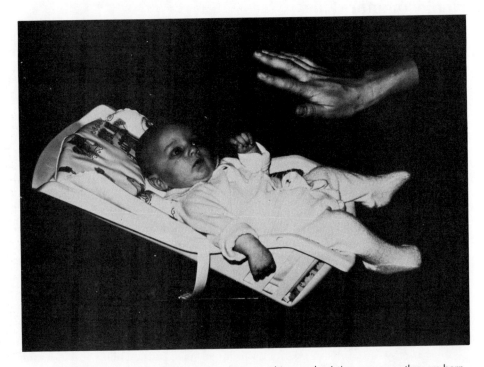

Fig. 6-26. Infants begin reflexively bending, stretching, and twisting as soon as they are born.

are not moving from place to place makes these skills very effective learning media for body and spatial concepts. You will soon discover various ways to provide these kinds of learning experiences if you maintain the attitude that every activity contains learning potential.

BENDING AND STRETCHING

When you see the child reaching up to the counter to get something, imitate his reaching movements while verbalizing the fact that he is stretching. You can then point out the difference between bending and stretching while modeling these actions. Begin with the concept of the child's total body as a bending and stretching instrument. An activity of this type might progress as follows:

Look at you stretching up to the counter. I am going to stretch up, too! Let's stretch together. Stretch up!

Now let's bend down to the floor. Do you want to talk while we are bending? (*Response.*) Let's stretch again. (Increase the speed as you continue bending and stretching.)

When the child demonstrates the ability to associate bending and stretching skills with the movements of his body, and when he has become familiar with the words "bending" and "stretching," you can use these skills

Fig. 6-27. Children bend and stretch as they climb and explore spaces.

to develop body and spatial awareness concepts. Activities of this nature could progress as follows:

I have an idea; let's bend and stretch parts of our body. Let's stretch our arm; bend our arm; stretch, bend, stretch, bend. Let's stretch our legs; bend our legs; stretch, bend, stretch, bend. Stretch our finger; bend our finger. (Continue until the child appears ready for a change of activity.)

The following list illustrates other kinds of activities that can be utilized in concept development:

Bend forward; bend backward; bend sideways.

Stretch up high; bend down low.

Stretch and make yourself big.

Bend and make yourself little.

Stretch your legs wide apart.

Stretch and bend your arm very fast, then faster; very slow, then slower.

Let's stretch inside the box, then outside the box.

Bend and walk through the box.

Bend over the box.

Bend our arms and walk around the box.

Can you bend my arm? I'll bend your arm.

Can you bend my knees? I'll bend your knees.

You can create a number of additional activities by combining bend and stretch with the locomotor movements of running and jumping.

PUSHING AND PULLING

With a large number of push-and-pull toys now available for young children, the opportunity to introduce these skills is always present. When an opportunity arises, introduce the skills of pushing and pulling by pointing out the difference between them. One way of doing this is to use a rolling toy the child enjoys (such as a car or truck). By using an object on wheels, the child can clearly see that when you push the object, it goes away from you, and when you pull the object, it comes back toward you. You can also relate the concepts of *pushing* and *away* with the concept of "far," and the concept of *pulling* with the concepts of *toward* and *close*. The following examples illustrate a possible progression.

Begin with you and the child sitting on the floor far enough apart so that you can roll a car back and forth between you. Ask the child to push the toy and, as the toy leaves the child's hand, verbalize for the child by saying, "You pushed the car and there it goes away from you. It's going far away. Wave bye-bye to the car; you pushed it away and it's going far away." Roll the car back to the child and verbalize, "Now catch the car." As soon as the child grasps the car say, "Now pull it close to you. Do you like your car? (*Response.*) Pull it close." Next you can say, "Ready, push it away. There it goes." Repeat the activity until the child appears to lose interest. This is a

Fig. 6-28. Push and pull toys provide excellent skill practice.

good introductory activity, but to reinforce the concepts of push and pull you need an activity in which the time between the push and the pull is limited. For example, obtain a car, a truck, and several balls. Position yourself beside the child with both of you facing a wall. Position yourselves so that if the child stretches, she can touch the wall but only if she stretches far. Hand the child a car and have her push it away so it strikes the wall. Then tell her to pull it close. As the child grasps the car ask, "Is it hurt?" Then let the child respond. Repeat the action, again asking the child, "Is it hurt?" Next change the object from a car to a truck and then to a ball. Continue to verbally emphasize, "Push away and pull close."

Another fun-filled activity that will enable the child to visualize the object going away and coming back involves a riding toy. Tie a rope to the

Fig. 6-29. Adults can assist a child to develop the concept of pulling with the hands and arms.

Fig. 6-30. Tugging on a rope is a challenging pulling activity.

riding toy and hold onto the end of the rope. Have the child push the toy with enough force to cause it to travel the distance of the length of the rope. Verbally emphasize this point. Then give the rope to the child and have him pull the riding toy back toward himself. Repeat the activity until the child is ready for a change. Children tend to back up to pull the object toward them. You can assist the child in developing the concept of pulling with the hands and arms by positioning yourself behind him and challenging him to "pull" (Fig. 6-29).

When the child has begun to associate the concepts of push and pull, you can point out the push and pull activities you see the child perform during the day. For example, at the dinner table the child may push his plate away when finished eating or pull it close when asking for more, or while diapers are being changed the child may push you away then pull you close for a kiss. Once the child has some basic understanding of the skills of pushing and pulling, begin using these skills to enhance body and spatial awareness. Examples of these kinds of activities are as follows:

Try to push the wall away with your hands (head, foot, or bottom). Does the wall move away? (*Response.*) Try to push the box away with your hands (head, foot, elbows, or knees). Does the box move away when you push it? (*Response.*)

Try to pull the box close to you with your hands; push it; pull it.

Can you push me; pull me; push my hands; pull my hands; push on my middle; pull my arm? (Reverse roles and push and pull various parts of the child's body.)

Push the car and make it go backward.

Pull the car and make it go forward.

I'll push you and make you go backward. Now you push me.

I'll pull you close to me and make you come toward me. Now you pull me.

Push the big truck away.

Pull the little car close to you.

Push the truck inside the garage.

Pull the truck outside the garage.

Push the truck around the garage.

You can create additional activities by combining pushing and pulling with the locomotor movements of walking and running.

SWINGING AND ROCKING

Swinging is a circular or arclike movement of a body part around a stationary center point. The only body parts with a structure that permits them to swing freely in full circles are the arms. The legs can swing one at a time in an arclike motion. The upper trunk and head can also swing, but their range of motion is limited. Rocking is a sustained movement of the entire body from side to side or forward and backward.

Fig. 6-31. An adult can assist a child to maintain a balanced position while learning to rock.

Swinging and rocking are fairly easy skills to execute because they require minimal strength and balance. Children frequently execute these skills; therefore, our goal is to assist them to become aware of what they are doing and to form associations between these and other actions.

Introduce the skills of swinging and rocking, using the imitation technique. Verbalize constantly, assisting the child to make associations between the words and the experiences. Swinging and rocking are rhythmical movements, so music or singing can be effectively used as accompaniment. We discovered that some modified verses to the tune of "Swing Low, Sweet Chariot" work well. It might go like this:

> Swing your arms,
> Sweet baby Becky (*child's name*),
> I'm coming forth to kiss your nose;
> Swing your leg,
> Sweet baby Becky,
> Coming over to grab your toes.

As you can tell, this is an original song that was composed on the spur of the moment, and you can do it too. Changing the words of a traditional song is easy. Children love music, and once you try it, their enthusiasm and enjoyment will keep you going.

For rocking we used such traditional songs as "Rock-a-Bye Baby" and "Rocking Your Baby in the Bosom of Abraham," (Rock My Soul in the Bosom of Abraham)—nothing spectacular, but highly successful none the less!

Once the child has become a real "swinger and rocker," you should use these skills as a medium for concept learning. Nonlocomotor movements are inherent parts of some locomotor movements. For example, we bend our knees in preparation to stretch or jump. We swing our arms when walking, running, and striking, and swing our leg when we kick. Children continuously execute nonlocomotor and locomotor movements in combinations, so our task is to assist them to develop an awareness of these associations. In the progressions we have presented in this chapter, the child has been introduced to jumping and bending separately. However, as you begin emphasizing concept learning, you should point out that bending the knees is essential in a jump. Verbalizing these kinds of associations builds a foundation for immediate as well as future relational thought.

Swinging plays an important role in several locomotor and manipulative activities such as walking, running, throwing, striking, and kicking. If the child has been introduced to all of these skills, he is ready to make the association between swinging and these locomotor manipulative movements. To do this you simply exaggerate the movements as you model and verbalize the actions. For example

Swing your arm and strike the ball.

Swing your leg and kick.

Swing your arm and roll the ball.

As you read the information concerning the manipulative skills (pp. 151-170), note how a great deal of emphasis is placed on swinging movements.

Rocking can also be combined with locomotor movements. For example

Rock and walk.

Rock and run.

Rock and jump.

Rock, gallop, and then rock.

Once the child has experienced swinging and rocking, these skills can be used to reinforce body and spatial concepts. For example, in developing body awareness

Swing your leg.

Swing one arm; two arms.

Swing your head (trunk).

Rock on your feet.

Put your hands on your hips and rock.

Put your hands on your head and rock.

Hold my hands and rock.

Hold my hips and rock.

A fun-filled activity that can be used with many skills is hand painting. Place an outline of a person on the wall. Have the child dip his hand in a shallow container full of the paint used for making handprints. (This paint

Fig. 6-32. Striking a ball involves swinging the arm while twisting the body.

can be made from edible materials such as ketchup or pudding, or you may use any of the nontoxic commercial paints made especially for children.) Have the child swing his arms and touch or strike different parts of the outlined body. If you want to encourage the child to control his natural urge to just randomly splatter the paint, you can count the movements. A count of three works well. It goes like this: one, dip your hand in the paint; two, swing your arms; and three, strike the head. Repeat the activity until either you or the child has had enough. Remember that if the paint is too runny, it will splatter all over the room, so keep it relatively thick. Thicker paint also makes clearer handprints because the paint doesn't drip on the picture. As you can see, it may be preferable to use this as an outdoor activity.

The following examples illustrate how swinging and rocking can be used to emphasize spatial and temporal (time) concepts:

Rock and walk backward (or forward).

Rock from side to side.

Rock back and forth.

Rock and walk up the ramp (or down the ramp).

Swing your leg inside a box (or outside a box, on top of a box, or under a box).

Swing your arms and run around a box.

Swing your arms in big circles (or little circles).

Stop-and-go activities (swing and stop or rock and stop).

Swing your arms hard.

Swing your leg fast.

Rock fast, then faster and faster.

TWISTING AND TURNING

A twist is a rotation of the body or a body part around a long axis. When you twist, your feet do not move. A turn is a movement in which the body or certain body parts are rotated. When the entire body is turned, the base of support must shift from one position to another. In other words, the feet turn as the body turns.

Introduce the skills of twisting and turning by having the child imitate you as you twist and turn your body parts and your body as a whole. Children particularly enjoy turning because it produces a state of dizziness.

When the child has experienced twisting and turning and is familiar with the words, you can introduce body awareness activities by having her twist and turn certain body parts. You can also use these skills to teach spatial and temporal dimensions. For example

Twist up high.

Twist down low.

Turn up high.

Turn down low.

Twist inside a box.

Twist outside a box.

Turn fast, faster, faster, and stop.

Turn and stomp your feet hard (or soft).

Finally, combine the skills of twisting and turning with other locomotor and manipulative skills. When you do this, spatial concepts may also be included. For example

Run and turn.

Walk and twist.

Run backward and turn.

Jump and turn.

RISING AND FALLING

Rising and falling are familiar movements in the life of the young child. Learning to move involves developing the strength and balance that enable the child to cope with the constant struggle against the force of gravity. As this struggle progresses, the young child constantly experiences rising and falling. Later when the child executes more complex locomotor skills, she must master body positions that are momentarily unstable. The inability to maintain body control in these situations will again cause the child to lose her balance and fall. As the child gains more and more control of her own body and can enjoy activities requiring body mastery, falling and rising become skills that are fun to purposely execute and practice.

Introduce falling and rising by using the imitation technique (pp. 39-41). Begin with whole body activities, such as the whole body falling from a standing position and then rising to standing again. Or you may want to begin with the whole body falling from a kneeling position and then rising to the same position. As soon as the child recognizes falling and rising as specific movements, you can begin combining them with other concepts. Examples of these activities follow.

Activities to develop body awareness

> While in sitting, standing, or lying positions, hold your arms up and let them fall.
> Raise your arms slowly and let them fall.
> Let your head fall forward, then raise it up.
> Hold your leg up and let it fall.
> Put your hand on your nose and let it fall.
> Raise my arm up and let it fall.
> Raise my leg up and let it fall.

Activities to develop spatial awareness

> Let your body fall forward, backward, or sideways.
> While standing up high, fall down.
> While squatting down low, fall down.
> Fall inside a box.
> Fall and rise fast, then faster and faster.

Combine fall and rise with other nonlocomotor movements as well as locomotor and manipulative skills. For example

> Bend down and fall.
> Walk and fall.
> Run and fall.
> Jump and fall.
> Stretch up and fall.
> Turn and fall.

Remember, it is possible to form endless combinations of concepts and skills. Not only can you combine skills with concepts, but you can also combine skills with skills and concepts with concepts. Once you grasp this basic idea, a new world of meaning and experiencing will open up to you and the child.

Manipulative skills

Manipulative skills are more complex than locomotor and nonlocomotor skills. Locomotor and nonlocomotor skills involve only two factors: the child and space. Manipulative skills involve three factors: the child, an object, and space.

The manipulative skills of catching and tossing are usually practiced together. However, to clarify our discussion of the teaching progression, we will treat them separately and then combine them in certain activities.

The child should play with different balls varying in size and weight. Balls should range from small enough to fit in one hand to the largest beach ball you can find. Sponge balls are edible, so if you select these be sure to watch the child carefully.

CATCHING

We call the child's first catching activity "fetching." This involves the child locating a ball, picking it up, and bringing it to you through some means. By varying this basic activity, you can assist the child in developing the visual tracking and hand-eye coordination necessary for more advanced skills. The first thing you must remember is that *young children cannot catch a ball thrown at them*. Notice we said *at* them, and this is literally

Fig. 6-33. Bouncing a ball back and forth provides practice in visual tracking.

what we mean. When a young child is required to receive a thrown object, he actually becomes a live target someone is trying to hit. If this is true, you may well ask "Why include catching at all?" Catching is a difficult skill with many prerequisite skills that are not specific to the skill of catching. Actually the skills necessary for catching are the same as those for reading and writing, namely, visual tracking and hand-eye coordination. Catching requires an additional prerequisite skill, that is, an awareness of the body in space. These skills must be developed through constant practice, and ball-handling activities provide an ideal medium.

Fetching involves locating a stationary ball and gaining control of it by grasping. After the child has practiced this initial step, he should progress to locating and following a moving ball and grasping it after it stops. Simply roll the ball and have the child chase it. At first try to roll the ball so it will stop before the child gets to it because this eliminates those little frustrations that may discourage the child and prevent him from wanting to repeat the activity.

When the child appears to have mastered gaining control of a rolling ball, progress to tossing the ball and having it bounce slightly. Remember to vary the spatial dimensions by tossing it forward, sideward and backward.

After extensive practice the child will be ready to stop a moving ball. It is best to begin this activity with the child in a sitting position. Sit opposite the child and roll the ball back and forth. Watch the child's eyes as the ball is approaching her and see if she is attempting to visually track it. Vary the activity so that the child will be required to watch the ball. Some of the variations you can use are as follows:

1. Roll the ball to one side of the child and then to the other side instead of to the child's midline.
2. Bounce the ball slightly.
3. Spin the ball as you roll it.
4. Have several balls behind your back and change balls when it is your turn, varying the size and color.
5. Put pieces of tape on the ball, and when the child catches the ball, let her pull the tape off.

When the child becomes proficient at stopping the ball while sitting, progress to standing, repeating the activities just described. If the child continues to be successful, use rolling and stopping activities as a learning medium for concepts. Begin with body awareness activities, using imitation techniques. Have the child stop the ball with different body parts such as her feet, knees, and elbows.

Next introduce the spatial dimensions. Have the child roll the ball forward. Then both of you can turn back to back and stand with your legs wide apart. Roll the ball backward, back and forth between your legs.

To introduce levels, have the child hold the ball up high or down low after he has stopped and grasped it. To introduce size, roll two balls to the child, one big and one small, while saying, "Catch the big (or small) ball." Be sure to reward these attempts or successes with love!

Using a "play object," introduce the child to spatial relationships. The following activities utilize the 36 × 36 × 36 inch wooden square with ramps pictured in Fig. 6-11.

1. Have the child stand inside the box. Roll the ball to the child, challenging him to catch it. Then have the child roll the ball outside to you. Repeat this inside-outside sequence. Remember to verbalize the action of the ball and the spatial relationships of inside-outside.
2. You and the child stand on opposite sides of the box, rolling the ball through the box and catching it each time.
3. In the same position as in 2, alternate rolling the ball over the box,

Fig. 6-34. Following the movement of a suspended ball involves visual tracking.

rolling it through the box, and then rolling it under the ramps on each side, attempting to catch it each time.

4. Have the child stand on top of the box while you stand at the bottom of the ramp. Roll the ball up to the child, challenging him to catch it and roll it back down. Repeat, changing sides. Then change places with the child. The child may have trouble getting the ball up the ramp at first, but will quickly catch on and push the ball *hard*. The ball will also roll down the ramp fast. Point this out and emphasize the contrast of fast versus slow whenever it occurs.

Because you will be limited in the amount of time you can spend with the child on a one-to-one basis, it will be necessary to devise activities that the child can do by herself. Rolling the ball against a wall is one of these activities. Simply show the child that she can roll the ball against the wall and it will come back. Have the child sit, facing the wall with her legs wide apart. Challenge her to roll the ball against the wall and catch it after it rebounds. Vary the activity by having her

Roll it fast; then faster and faster.

Roll it and stop it with the elbows and fingertips.

Trap it between the legs or under the chin.

After the child has some experience in handling the ball on the ground, suspend a large ball (10 inches in diameter) from a clothesline, a tree, or a doorway. Adjust the height of the ball so it is hanging at the level of the child's arms. Show the child how to push the ball and try to catch it when it comes back. Encourage the child to watch the ball. You can do this by taping pictures on the ball. Family pictures are fun because you can "push Mommy" or "catch Daddy."

TOSSING

When tossing, the motion of the body is directly transferred to an object held in one or both hands. The speed and direction in which the hand is moving at the moment the object is released determines the speed, direction, and distance the object will travel. Note the complexity that is involved in the previous statement. The child must coordinate her total body, transfer the motion to an object, and be aware of the cause-and-effect relationship between herself and the space in which she is moving. When you consider all that is involved, it is evident why it takes many years of practice and instruction to develop a mature throwing pattern. And it is also apparent why you should not attempt to teach children younger than 2 years of age to execute a mature throwing pattern. Rather as continually emphasized, you should prepare children for later, more complex learning by using a beginning skill such as tossing.

As in all other skills, rudimentary forms of tossing begin early in life. A tossing pattern actually begins when the child learns to release an object. Releasing later becomes dropping. The distinction is that dropping is releasing the ball with a purpose (that is, to hit the ground). Dropping eventually evolves into tossing.

DROPPING

Dropping activities play an essential role in the development of the child's construction of reality, especially in areas dealing with cause and effect. Dropping activities play this important role because they enable the child to make associations between movement and space.

Most toddlers will soon become proficient at dropping, so you can begin utilizing this skill in concept development immediately. Do not, however, assume that the child has mastered the skill of dropping. Introduce it by using the imitation technique, and if the child is immediately successful, move on; if not, practice the skill.

Activities to develop body awareness

Have the child hold a ball with different body parts; then have the child drop it. Vary the size of the ball. Challenge the child to catch the ball after it bounces. (When we say "catch" we mean locate the ball and pick it up.)

Progress to the following activities in which both you and the child have a ball. Using a large, light ball (approximately 10 inches in diameter)

Drop the ball with two hands.

Drop the ball with your elbows. (The child may need assistance in positioning the ball. However, let him ask for help; otherwise, just be patient.)

Drop the ball with your knees.

Bend at the waist, holding the ball between the chest and hips; then straighten up and let the ball drop.

Using a small ball

Drop the ball with one hand.

Drop the ball with your chin.

Drop the ball from under your armpit.

Drop the ball from between your knees.

Ask the child questions following this progression:

Question	Response
Did the ball go down after you dropped it?	Yes
Does the ball go up or down when you drop it?	Down
What happens to the ball when you drop it?	Falls
Falls where?	Down

The purpose of asking these questions is to stimulate the child to make an association between dropping the ball and the direction down. Therefore you will need to continue this guided conversation until you reach the correct answer.

Fig. 6-35. Dropping a ball over the head develops body and spatial awareness.

Another body awareness game that is slightly more difficult because the action occurs outside the child's visual field is the Drop, Turn, and Catch game. The game consists of dropping the ball behind you and turning around to retrieve the ball. Introduce the game using the imitation technique. Vary the size of the ball and the manner that the ball gets behind the child. For example drop the ball behind you by putting the ball

Over your head
Over your shoulder
Down behind your back
Between your legs

Vary the game by having the child face you, and take turns catching each other's ball as it drops behind. For example, drop the ball behind you; the

Fig. 6-36. Holding a ball up high and dropping it into a bucket of water are novel tasks.

child then runs around you (or through your legs) and catches the ball. Then the child takes a turn, and you catch the ball by going around the child (or reaching through his legs or over him). Always positively reinforce the child's efforts.

Activities to develop spatial awareness

The following examples illustrate how dropping can be used as a spatial concept learning medium.

Hold the ball *high* and let it drop *big*.

Hold the ball *low* and let it drop *little*.

Using various play objects have the child

Drop the ball *over* the box or any other object.

Drop the ball *inside* the box, then *outside* the box.

Drop the ball *close* to the box.

These examples are merely guides to stimulate your thinking; you can combine many of these. For example, the child can get up on top of the box and drop the ball inside a bucket. Any number of combinations are possible; so try it, you'll like it!

Another fun-filled variation of dropping is knocking objects over. Blocks are great, but you can use any object that will tip over. If you watch the child's nonverbal communication, you can almost see her thinking, "I caused that to happen." Introduce the knocking down activity by dropping a ball on top of the objects; then let the child repeat the action as long as it holds her interest.

ROLLING

Rolling begins as a push; the child pushes a ball, usually with two hands. Then as the child practices, he progresses to a one-handed push. Eventually his refined rolling pattern will consist of swinging one or both arms and releasing the ball.

Introduce the child to rolling while he is sitting down. Then when he can control the ball, progress to standing up. Use the imitation technique with both of you participating in lots of practice.

The child can sit with his legs together and practice rolling the ball down his legs, then raise his feet and try to catch the ball. The child may prefer rolling the ball on your legs because they are longer; this seems more exciting to the child. The child can also practice rolling the ball up and down inclines. You can add variety to this task by letting him knock something over at the bottom. You can also try rolling the ball down a balance beam, down the steps, or down the child's entire body while he is leaning against the house or sofa.

When the child becomes proficient at rolling, you should use the skill in activities that assist him in making associations. These kinds of activities are included in the section dealing with catching. By reviewing these activities, you can gain the insight necessary for developing additional practice situations for rolling.

TOSSING

A rolling ball stays on the ground, whereas a tossed ball travels in the air. The body motion is the same for both skills but the release is different. To successfully execute the skill of tossing, the child must make an association between the direction of the release and the flight of the ball. It is essential for her to know that if her arm goes up, the ball also goes up. The most vital aspect of the child's learning in this situation is the insight she is developing about what causes specific changes. Remember that the *constructing a reality* aspect of the child's development enabled her to conceive

Fig. 6-37. Children sense feelings of power and control when they execute cause-and-effect actions.

of herself as an object in space capable of causing change. This ability has to be developed. The child must internalize the answers to the questions: What is my body? What is this space? How do I cause change by moving my body in this space?

The skill of tossing involves the nonlocomotor movement of swinging the arm. Introduce the child to tossing by using the imitation technique while verbalizing in a way that will emphasize the arm swing. Provide lots of practice time. As the child makes more and more associations, her practice will vary considerably. The child will naturally begin to explore body and spatial concepts as she becomes aware of her movement potential.

When tossing becomes a proficient skill, begin emphasizing concept de-

Fig. 6-38. A, Children tend to walk up close to a target before throwing. **B,** Some toddlers throw with both arms at the same time.

velopment. Tossing does not always have to involve a ball. Bean bags and yarn balls provide nice texture variations and can lead to development of various activities.

A target of any kind can stimulate tossing practice. Use different colors and shapes or pictures of animals or body parts. You should be aware that the child will figure out that the way to hit the target is to walk right up to it and put the ball directly on it or to toss the ball while standing only about 8 inches away from the target. Therefore as the child continues to practice, try to get the child to stand back away from the target. This can be done in several ways:

Provide a line to stand on and to toss from.

Make the target larger.

Ask the child to stand back beside you.

Reward the child for throwing from the desired distance.

Have her toss the ball, and then listen for it to hit the target.

Providing a variety of targets stimulates practice. Targets that make loud noises are extremely rewarding (for example, aluminum pie pans or wind chimes). Another fun activity for warm weather is tossing a ball into a large bucket of water and seeing the splash. A soft throw makes a little splash and a hard throw makes a big splash.

There is no need whatsoever for a young child to begin tossing a ball with an overhand pattern. However, it is commonplace in our society for adults to force children to become little ballplayers. Young children are not capable of developing refined movement patterns. Rather, they should explore a wide variety of movement possibilities and develop the concepts that will enable them to make cause-and-effect relationships.

STRIKING

Striking is a swinging motion in which force is imparted to an object for the purpose of propelling it through space. A body part or an implement is used to strike a stationary or moving object. It is easier to strike a stationary object because the child is not required to judge the speed and direction in which the object is moving. Kicking is a form of striking, but this skill will be discussed separately, since the child must balance his body in a different way to kick.

Introduce the skill of striking through imitation. The introductory activity involves swinging the arm and striking a light, large ball (10 inches or more in diameter) that is lying on the ground. Provide lots of practice. When the child becomes bored with self-initiated practice, the following activity will stimulate renewed interest.

Swing your arm and strike the ball. Have the child run and chase the ball, striking it when he gets near it. Repeat the activity. Emphasize swinging the arm and striking the ball hard.

To introduce the association between the concept of direction and strik-

Fig. 6-39. Children enjoy striking a large ball.

ing the ball toward a target, begin striking the ball to the child and having the child strike the ball back to you. As you strike the ball to the child, carefully judge the distance so that the ball will stop before it reaches the child. This provides the child with a stationary rather than a moving target. If the ball does not stop or if the child wants to get in the act sooner, let her run to it, stop its motion, and strike it. Again, the most effective way to convey the message of the desired action is through imitation. Simply model this by pointing out that you stop the ball before you strike it. Be sure to verbalize all the actions in a repetitive manner. For example, when the ball comes to you, verbalize "stop" and "strike." Be sure to use the terms *strike* or *striking* rather than *hit* or *hitting*. Striking is the word the child should learn to associate with this body action. It is incorrect to refer to it as hitting the object. Also it is undesirable to encourage the child to view "hitting" anything as an acceptable action.

As soon as the child has made the association between striking and swinging her arm at the ball, it is time to move on to using this skill as a medium for concept development.

Activities to develop body awareness

Introduce body awareness activities by having the child strike the ball with different body parts. The association you desire for the child to make is the awareness that, "I can strike with my body parts." For example

Strike the ball with one arm.

Strike the ball with two arms.

Strike the ball with one elbow.

Strike the ball with the head.

Strike the ball with one foot (kick).

Striking with one foot is kicking. This skill will be discussed separately in the next section.

Activities to develop spatial awareness

Using the skill of swinging the arm and striking the ball enables the child to study concepts relative to direction. The following activities illustrate these kinds of learning situations.

Strike the ball forward, starting with your arm behind you. (Exaggerate the starting position of your arm in your modeling procedures, and verbalize, "Arm in back," "Swing forward," and "Strike forward.")

Strike the ball backward, starting with your arm in front of you. (Exaggerate this starting position and verbalize, "Arm in front," "Swing backward," and "Strike backward.")

Strike the ball sideways, starting with your arm to the side. (Repeat the procedure as just described.)

Participation in these activities is laying the foundation for the association that will enable the child to relate the direction of the force (swing of the arm) with the direction the ball will travel. These concepts are rather difficult so progress slowly and be patient.

It may be easier for the child to make the association that swinging the arm upward as he strikes the ball causes the ball to go up high. And, conversely, swinging the arm downward and striking the ball cause the ball to go down.

Begin by holding the ball while the child attempts to strike it. This can be a bit hazardous, so we suggest you position yourself so your head does not become the target. Have the child start with his arm positioned downward and then swing it up to strike the ball. As the child strikes the ball, allow it to leave your hand and travel upward. If the child applies a great deal of force, he may not be able to track the ball because it will rapidly leave his visual field. Therefore you should always verbally reinforce the fact the ball went up. Review the action by asking the child where the ball went. Encourage the child to strike the ball hard because the resulting action will emphasize the association between the amount of force and the motion of the ball.

Repeat this activity, using a downward swing. Have the child start with his arm up and swing downward, causing the ball to go down. Position yourself appropriately so you will not interfere with the flight of the ball. When you introduce this activity, it will be easier if you have another adult or an older child demonstrate the movements. This will enable the child to stand back and to watch the action prior to becoming involved in it.

Make various shapes with your body and have the child do the same. Strike the ball under or through the holes formed by your body parts. For example, the child can stand with his legs wide apart and strike the ball backward between his legs or the two of you can play in partners. To play in partners, you make a shape and the child strikes the ball under and through the hole in your body shape. Then the child makes a shape and you strike the ball under and through.

When the child can successfully strike the ball on the ground, suspend the ball as shown in Figs. 6-40 and 6-41. This gives the child the opportunity to track the ball continuously. If the child is having trouble striking the ball because of its continual motion, show the child how to stop the ball and then strike it. This then becomes a catch-and-strike activity.

We have described how the child should be introduced to striking by using her hands. When she has become familiar with this skill, she is ready to progress to striking with an implement.

When a child holds a striking implement such as a small paddle or plastic bat, it has the effect of lengthening the body lever. This means the child must develop the ability to spatially relate the extended lever to the object she is attempting to strike. Not only must the child control the added length of the implement, but she must also relate to its additional size and weight. Therefore in the beginning it is essential to have a small, light, short implement. We use plastic bowling pins because of their size, weight, length, and availability. Small plastic bats are also good.

To introduce striking with an implement, first use a ball on the ground and then progress to a suspended ball. At first the child will hold the implement in one hand and chop at the ball. Just let him practice striking the ball whatever way he chooses. Remember, no matter how he executes the skill, he is learning visual tracking and hand-eye coordination. After some daily practice, you can encourage the child to place two hands on the bat and use more of a swing. The child may try this on his own, and you can then reinforce the attempt. If the child reverts to a one-handed swing, just be patient and return to a two-handed position when he appears ready. Midline activities such as this are difficult for young children. However, when the time is right for the child, he will use two hands, so keep trying. A child will usually (but not always) begin using two hands as soon as he becomes an efficient one-handed striker.

Once the child has acquired some basic control over an implement, you can use striking skills to reinforce concept development. The striking activities we have described offer the opportunity for the child to form associations between

1. Striking and swinging body parts
2. Striking and swinging implements
3. Striking and direction
4. Striking and levels

5. Striking and shapes

6. Striking and other people's body positions

Next you might progress to striking and the concept of size. The child can strike small balls or large balls. As you work with the child and become alert to the possibilities presented by different kinds of equipment, you will be able to create other combinations of concepts.

The next learning level involves forming associations between striking and other objects such as a target. This level is the most difficult because it involves relating oneself to the striking object, then relating the struck object to another object.

You can initiate these kinds of activities by having the child strike a ball

Fig. 6-40. Striking an object with an implement increases the complexity of the skill.

toward a target. For example, using the wooden square play object with ramps (Fig. 6-11), you can have the child

Strike the ball so it goes inside the box.

Stand inside the box and strike the ball so it goes to the outside.

Strike the ball through the box.

Strike the ball under the ramp.

Strike the ball over the ramp.

Strike the ball down the ramp.

Strike the ball up the ramp.

This can be done with an implement or different body parts. Introduce each of these skills to the child or observe while the child introduces them

Fig. 6-41. Striking a Ping-Pong ball with a paddle is an interesting activity because it makes a noise.

to you because he may discover them through exploration. When the child does discover a new activity, you should imitate him and use the opportunity to reinforce the associations the child has discovered.

Finally introduce the child to the concept that the object one strikes can strike something else. For example, strike a ball against a wall or backboard of some type. If the child experiences difficulty, have him stop the ball before attempting to strike it. The side of a building or a wall makes a nice big target. You can add interest by placing a large body shape on the wall and challenging the child to strike the ball toward different body parts. You can also use targets that differ in color and shape. When using target activities make sure the child will be successful by providing large targets located close to the ground. In such a situation the child will be required only to relate to the direction in which the ball travels and not to the height of the ball. Most struck balls will stay fairly close to the ground.

You can add variety by elevating the ball. You can do this by using small traffic cones. Children enjoy putting the ball on the cone and then striking it. This activity contains the additional challenge of requiring the hand-eye coordination necessary to balance the ball on top of the cone. If you analyze this activity, you can see that it requires the use of many skills. The child strikes the ball, runs after the ball, catches the ball, returns it to the cone,

Fig. 6-42. Using traffic cones enables the child to strike an elevated stationary object.

balances the ball in the cone, and repeats the sequence. This analysis conveys how a step-by-step progression is followed to teach related skills that can then be combined to form a challenging, complex learning activity.

KICKING

Kicking is a relatively difficult skill because balance must be maintained on a small base of support (one foot) while the swinging leg imparts force to the ball. You will be able to observe this difficulty if you ask your child to stand on one foot. Your child will probably respond by raising the nonsupport foot to a tiptoe position and then attempting to raise the leg. The action of raising the leg will probably appear more like the nonsupport foot tapping the floor. The child will probably solve this problem by finding something to hold onto and showing you, "See, I can do it."

Most children who are approaching age 2 have gained enough leg strength and the sense of balance necessary to stand on one foot. They should practice this skill daily. It only takes a few seconds, and the practice effects are soon noticeable. Not only is this skill essential in kicking, but being able to stand on one foot is prerequisite to the more complex locomotor skills of hopping and skipping.

The most effective way to initiate the skill of kicking is to stimulate the

Fig. 6-43. With practice young children can become skillful kickers.

child to introduce the skill to you. The first kicking you will notice is a push kick. While walking the child will naturally push the ball as the nonsupport leg swings through to take another step. Once the child makes contact with the ball by using her foot, simply reinforce the action by assisting the child in making the association between the word *kicking* and the action of striking the ball with the foot.

Provide plenty of opportunities for the child to practice the skill of kicking. Encourage her to run and kick the ball. Quite often a child will run and kick a ball repeatedly throughout the entire yard. Encourage the child to kick the ball hard. Begin laying a foundation for the association between the force imparted to the ball and the distance the ball travels.

After the child has experienced kicking a ball on the ground, suspend the ball from a tree, clothesline, or ceiling. Suspend it at a position just off the ground or floor. The child can then participate in concentrated, uninterrupted kicking practice that will develop tracking skills and foot-eye coordination. If the child experiences difficulty, demonstrate a way to stop the ball before kicking it.

Once kicking becomes a relatively proficient skill (as evidenced by the child's continued success in imparting force to the ball and causing it to travel through space), use the skill of kicking as a medium for concept development. Most of the activities described in the section devoted to striking are also applicable to kicking (pp. 161-167).

SWIMMING

Swimming is a manipulative skill. In this frame of reference we are looking at water as an object within the total space rather than as a separate water space. It is not within the scope of this book to provide you with a theoretical discussion of infant swimming or a detailed program outline. However, we would like to emphasize that swimming as a movement skill, like all other movement skills, can and must be used as a medium for concept development. The following examples illustrate this.

Activities to develop body awareness

Have the child move different body parts in the water and out of the water. For example
Move your finger in the water, then out of the water.
Move your feet in the water, then out of the water.
Move your shoulders in the water, then out of the water.
Make a big splash with your hands (or feet).

Activities to develop spatial awareness

Kick your feet in front of you.
Kick your feet behind you.
Kick your feet out to the side.

Open and close your legs under the water, making them wide, then narrow.

Make a straight line in the water with a boat.

Make the boat go in circles.

Put your hand over the water, then under the water.

Bring your feet close to your body, then far away.

Activities to develop temporal awareness

Kick your feet—"go," then "stop."

Kick your feet fast, faster, faster, then slow.

Strike the water hard with your hand.

Strike the water soft with your elbow.

These are just a few examples of what can be done in the water as your child is becoming "water safe." Notice as you reread these examples that several combinations of concepts were mentioned. This is pointed out to illustrate how your awareness has increased now that you have acquired a movement language!

SUMMARY

A child's movement vocabulary is both verbal (concepts) and nonverbal (body actions). This vocabulary develops as the child learns both movement and language skills. The extent of this development depends on practice and on the child being encouraged to form associations and make relationships.

While practicing locomotor, nonlocomotor, and manipulative skills, there is ample opportunity for the child to develop cognitively as well. The child uses body parts to execute all motor skills. Therefore the opportunity to develop body awareness concepts is always present. All movement occurs in space, and as the child moves through space, she must relate to the objects and structures present in the environment. The child develops spatial awareness and a knowledge of spatial relationships by paying attention to and verbalizing these spatial concepts.

The young child's world is rich in learning potential. However, for this potential to be actualized, caregivers must be alert to the learning possibilities and assist the child in realizing these possibilities. This means that both the caregiver and the child must be actively involved in the learning situation.

SUGGESTED READINGS

Corbin, C.B. (Ed.). *A textbook of motor development* (2nd ed.). Dubuque, Iowa: Wm. C. Brown, Co., Publishers, 1980.

Espenschade, A.S., and Eckert, H.M. *Motor development* (2nd ed.). Columbus, Ohio: Charles E. Merrill, Publishing Co., 1980.

Koch, J. *Total baby development.* New York: Wyden Books, 1976.

Zaichkowsy, L.D., Zaichkowsky, L.B., and Martinek, T.J. *Growth and development: the child and physical activity.* St. Louis: The C.V. Mosby Co., 1980.

CHAPTER 7

A child's play-learn environment

Play is the young child's learning environment. Play activities provide a medium in which the child's basic physical skills develop as well as provide opportunities for him to explore and discover himself in relation to the world. This is why it is vitally important to structure a play environment that will stimulate a wide variety of developmental learning experiences. In addition to providing a variety of activities, the child's play-learn environment must also be adaptable. The young child's developmental needs change as new skills emerge and as his awareness increases. To meet these needs, his surroundings must be periodically altered to create new challenges and different sources of stimulation.

A play environment is ordinarily thought of as a place where children have access to toys and child-size furniture. We will extend the concept of a play environment to include time and space as well as objects and structures. We have discovered that in a world where people are frequently crowded together and where they are controlled by time schedules, it is essential to be aware of the young child's time and space needs.

TIME

A child needs time alone as well as time with others. She also needs to participate in self-initiated and self-directed activities as well as activities in which an adult serves as facilitator. One reason for this is that children must have an opportunity to develop independence and self-confidence. These feelings gradually develop as they do things by themselves and for themselves. A second reason is that children need time alone to rest, to be quiet, to gather in their "I," "me," and "mine," and to renew their inner beings.

To meet these needs, there must be times when other people do not interfere in the child's activities and when she is not obliged to interact with others or meet the demands imposed by the expectations of others. Children need to be free to do the things they want to do without being told what to do, how to do it, or how well they did it. In other words, they need time to organize, direct, and evaluate their own behavior. They need time to get away from the business of their daily lives and to get back in touch with that quiet place inside themselves. Enjoying time spent alone to ex-

Fig. 7-1. A, Play is the young child's learning environment. **B,** For children play is serious business. It is their way of life, a medium in which to learn.

Fig. 7-2. Children need time alone to collect themselves as well as to explore their world.

perience this quiet place of serenity is an important aspect of every child's development. If this ability is nurtured early, it may remain an important aspect of the individual's life. This is why it is vital for the adult who controls the child's schedule to remember this need for *self time* and *self space* and to create opportunities for this need to be met.

SPACE

A physically active child moves through spaces and moves in relation to objects. Objects and structures occupy space, thereby limiting and defining the spaces through which the child may move. Each of these objects has a *size* and a *shape*. When an object is placed in a room or in an outdoor play area, it has a *location*. Thus these three factors (the size, shape, and location of objects) determine the size and shape of the space through which the child may move. These three factors also determine the direction in which the child may move and the pathway he may follow. All these components become a part of the child's developing spatial awareness.

In the same way an activity can be changed by substituting a different toy or piece of equipment, it can also be altered by changing the available space. Thus by changing the location of a piece of furniture, you have altered the child's movement environment. By rearranging an entire room, you have created a totally new learning environment. Periodic change stimulates interest, but too much change may be overwhelming. This is why you must attend to the child's behaviors and modify the learning situation in accordance with her particular developmental needs.

Sometimes the child's interest can be renewed simply by going from one room into another or from indoors to outdoors. At other times a greater environmental change may be necessary. Thus it is important for you to be aware of the child's movement needs and also of the concepts the child must learn to relate to the world of space. So much of the child's learning rests on your ability to detect and utilize spatial differences such as small and large, wide and narrow, straight, curved, angular, and the other concepts listed in the Learning by Moving table (p. 100). There is a built-in reward in all of this for you, too. At the same time you are becoming alert to the child's need to recognize and to deal with these dimensions, you will also be enlarging and enriching your own view of the world.

PLAY OBJECTS

Play objects are anything a young child can handle, manipulate, or move through space. A play object may be a commercially manufactured toy, an ordinary household item, or a homemade toy.

Commercial toys

Companies such as Community Playthings, Fisher-Price, Gabriel, Kenner, Mattel, and Playskool produce a wide variety of developmental toys. However, there are several points you should consider before buying a toy.

Fig. 7-3. Planks make excellent play objects because children can handle, manipulate, and control them.

Fig. 7-4. By moving and rearranging planks, children learn about size, shape, and location.

Your first consideration is that the object must stimulate active learning rather than passive entertainment. Play objects should invite the child's participation by stimulating him to become involved with it. This means that the child must be able to manipulate the object rather than being manipulated by the toy. It is also important for the toy to be versatile so that it will stimulate a variety of movement responses. One aspect of versatility is the ways in which the object can be used in combination with other toys. Exploring these kinds of combinations assists the child in forming associations and making relationships.

A second consideration is the quality of the workmanship. Some toys are hastily produced from inferior materials. Poor quality is sometimes masked by bright colors or a coat of paint. For this reason you should carefully examine the toy to be sure it is safe, hygienic, and durable.

Finally, you must select toys that are age appropriate. Adults sometimes have a tendency to purchase toys that appeal to them rather than to the child. Some companies label their toys with descriptive information specifying the ages for which they were designed. However, these labels do not take into consideration a particular child's needs and interests.

Household items

Anything the child can grasp is a potential play object. Pans, lids, plastic glasses, cups and bottles, baskets, and eating utensils are common household items, which the child can grasp, manipulate, and explore. These objects stimulate actions such as banging, stacking, squeezing, and fitting together.

Safety is the main consideration in using household items as toys. These objects are designed to serve other purposes, so they must be carefully checked over before being given to the child. The object must be unbreakable and should have no sharp edges. Plastic bottles should not contain any liquid except water. Of course, all these objects should be clean because sooner or later the child will probably "taste" them.

Homemade toys

Making toys for a child enables the two of you to share in a special way. Adults sometimes hesitate to make things because they think "it won't be good enough." This is an adult concept; the child doesn't care. The child only cares about playing, preferably *with* you, and the toy need not be anything elaborate. Old socks can easily become hand puppets or sock balls. Other objects that are easy to make include rattles, bean bags, and yarn balls.

Larger types of homemade play equipment include steps, inclines, balance beams, carpet squares, tunnels, and boxes. Anything you and the child can move and rearrange can become a toy that teaches.

A play objects library

Collecting and using play objects can be thought of as similar to a library filled with books. A library usually contains books of all sizes and shapes with information on a wide variety of topics. The child's collection of play objects should be like a library. The objects should be varied in design, size, shape, and color. And these objects should stimulate the child to discover a variety of characteristics, associations, and relationships.

The following list contains suggestions about the kinds of play objects that can be included in a child's play object library. This list should be viewed as sources for ideas rather than as a list of requirements. Some of the best toys can be discovered in the home environment when you use your imagination and when you allow the child to explore freely.

Visual discrimination skills

Body shapes, body parts models, blocks, puzzles, wall decorations that vary in size, shape, color, and level

Locomotor skills

Climbing: ladders, steps, slides, boxes

Crawling: barrels, open-ended boxes, collapsible toy tunnels, improvised tunnels

Walking and running: ramps, pathways, footsteps, and challenge courses involving changes of direction and level

Jumping: steps, large wooden blocks, plastic or wooden boxes, springboards, pads, mattresses

Manipulative skills

Objects to toss: balls, yarn balls, sock balls, bean bags, plastic bottles

Objects that roll: balls, spools, hoops, tires

Objects for striking: wands, brooms, large plastic bats, plastic bowling pins

Objects to stack and arrange: boxes, blocks, boards, crates, planks, small sawhorses

Containers: wheelbarrows, wagons, pans, boxes, buckets, pitchers, cups

Riding and steering skills

Wheel toys such as wagons, wheelbarrows, miniature hand trucks, doll buggies, toy grocery carts, trucks, tractors

Balancing skills

Planks, balance beams, balance boards, carpet squares

Swinging and rocking skills

Rocking boats, tire swings, rope swings

PLAY STRUCTURES

Play structures are large pieces of equipment that stimulate children to execute gross motor skills such as balancing, climbing, crawling, hanging, and swinging. Play structures vary widely in size and design. The structure

Fig. 7-5. Children need balls of all sizes. Large balls provide experiences that differ from those with small balls.

Fig. 7-6. A plastic bottle and a homemade body shape become collector's items for a play objects library.

Fig. 7-7. A variety of balancing equipment is readily available.

may be designed with a single purpose in mind, such as a set of steps (Fig. 7-8), a balance beam (Fig. 7-9), or a large cube (see Fig. 6-27). Multipurpose structures are designed to provide several different kinds of movement challenges. Commercial structures of this type are commonly designed so that children can climb, slide, and swing. These commercial structures often fail to hold the young child's interest. One reason is that the movement possibilities presented by these structures are very limited. Thus the child soon becomes bored by the repetitious nature of the activity. A young child's interest is stimulated and maintained by things that change. Therefore, the best play structures are ones that stimulate a variety of different learning activities. Another reason ordinary play structures lose their appeal is because adults tend to convey the attitude that once the structure is assembled, they are finished with it. After adults assemble a play structure, they often expect children to entertain themselves. Children want adults to play with them. They enjoy the adult's attention and thrive on the reinforcement this provides. They also need the stimulation provided by an adult's insight. An attentive adult can usually think of different ways to vary the movement task so that the same structure can serve different functions.

One of the most important questions you would ask before selecting a play structure is, "How functional is it?" You should consider how many

Fig. 7-8. Climbing steps requires concentration and body control.

different kinds of movement activities the structure will stimulate. A child's play environment should include structures that invite her to execute locomotor, nonlocomotor, and manipulative skills as well as to explore all the spatial dimensions and relationships. One of the most important factors to consider is the potential for the child to manipulate play objects while moving in relation to the structure.

When a ladder is added to a set of stairs, it becomes a multipurpose structure (see Fig. 6-21). A ramp is an example of a simple structure that serves several functions (see Fig. 6-2). Children can jump from the end and land on the rubber-covered inner tube. They can also move objects or their bodies up and down the ramp in a variety of ways. A car tire (Fig. 7-10) is a versatile structure because children can move on, over, under, around, and

Fig. 7-9. A and **B,** Balance beams can be constructed in several different ways.

Fig. 7-10. You can build this play structure for the price of a few nuts and bolts.

Fig. 7-11. A bounding board can be made with tires.

through it. A bounding board made with tires (Fig. 7-11) is simple and yet effective because children can move under, around, and through it in addition to crawling, walking, and jumping on it. The surplus cable spool shown in Fig. 7-12 offers several movement possibilities. Planks and boards can also be added to create temporary play structures (see Fig. 6-38).

The structures shown in Figs. 7-13 to 7-16 fully illustrate the concept of multipurpose structures.* A basic structure made from rope and timbers (Fig. 7-13) stimulates children to climb and to hang in different ways (Fig. 7-14) as well as to practice manipulative skills and to develop spatial awareness (Fig. 7-15).

---

* These structures were designed by Becky Bailey.

Fig. 7-12. A little paint applied to a cable spool adds an exciting dimension to a play environment.

Fig. 7-13. This structure was originally a swing set. By putting the structure on its side and adding rope, a dynamic play environment was created.

Fig. 7-14. The activities of these children fully illustrate what can be done with a multipurpose structure.

Fig. 7-15. A, Placing the ball between the rope rungs requires spatial awareness. **B,** Once the ball is in place, a child can strike it with different body parts.

Fig. 7-16. A, This maze structure enables children to practice problem-solving skills by orienting themselves in space. **B,** The surface of any play structure can be utilized to provide learning activities for young children. **C,** Steering a wagon through narrow spaces and sharp turns is a challenging learning experience.

C

Fig. 7-16, cont'd. For legend see opposite page.

Unlimited movement possibilities are evoked by a structure such as the one shown in Fig. 7-16. This maze of alleys, corners, and spaces illustrates how physical activity stimulates concept development. Children can move their bodies and objects in a variety of ways as they relate to the spaces created by the design of the maze. And the colorful patterns painted on the walls provide an interesting way for children to explore concepts relative to size, shape, level, direction, and color.

These examples of well-designed play structures illustrate how careful planning can enable you to obtain maximum educational value for your investment. They also evidence the importance of designing structures that are both functional and versatile.

SAFETY

Safety should be a paramount consideration in developing a child's play-learn environment. A concern for the child's safety should guide the selection of both play objects and play structures. However, this is only the beginning. An environment is constantly changing for one reason or another. This means that the caregiver must maintain an alert attitude toward detecting potentially injurious situations. This does not imply overprotecting the child. Rather, it suggests child proofing the environment and then adequately supervising the child's play.

Child proofing consists of removing all potentially dangerous objects and substances. It also involves preventing the child from having access to things that are potentially injurious such as electrical outlets, bodies of water, objects that may break or splinter, and places where the child may be hurt if he falls.

Adults sometimes forget that young children have a natural tendency to explore and experiment with everything. They will poke, disassemble, and taste anything that interests them. This means that anything that is potentially injurious must be removed from the environment. This applies to outside as well as inside areas. You should check the yard often to be sure it does not contain mushrooms or other dangerous plants or berries. You should also check for ant hills and for other types of insects that bite and sting.

Providing a safe environment is largely a matter of thinking ahead. The caregiver must try to anticipate how the child will respond and to create places where he can enjoy freely exploring the wonders of his world.

SUMMARY

A child's play environment is made up of people, places, and things. The way caregivers interact with the child is the single, most important factor in this environment. A young child will quickly lose interest in any activity that does not include an interested person. Time is also an important factor. Children need time to be free to explore alone if they so desire, knowing that whatever they discover can be shared with a concerned adult when they re-enter their social world. The remaining components of the child's world are spaces, objects, and structures. These tangible aspects of the child's world should be thoughtfully planned and evaluated according to how they serve to stimulate learning. This is why it is important to envision the child's surroundings as his play-learn environment.

SUGGESTED READINGS

Baker, K.R. *Let's play outdoors*. Washington, D.C.: National Association for the Education of Young Children, 1966.

Frost, J.L., and Klein, B.L. *Children's play and playgrounds*. Boston: Allyn & Bacon, Inc., 1979.

Garland, K. and Kalkstein, K. *Smart toys for babies from birth to two*. New York: Harper Colophon Books, 1981.

Hewes, J.J. *Build your own playground*. Boston: Houghton Mifflin Co., 1974.

Mason, J. *The environment of play*. West Point, New York: Leisure Press, 1982.

Miller, P.L. *Creative outdoor play areas*. Englewood Cliffs, N.J.: Prentice-Hall, Inc., 1972.

Werner, P.H., and Rini, L. *Perceptual-motor development equipment: inexpensive ideas and activities*. New York: John Wiley & Sons, Inc., 1976.

Werner, P.H., and Simmons, R. *Inexpensive physical education equipment for children*. Minneapolis: Burgess Publishing Co., 1976.

Bibliography

Baker, K.R. *Let's play outdoors*. Washington, D.C.: National Association for the Education of Young Children, 1966.

Braga, L., and Braga, J. *Children and adults; activities for growing together*. Englewood Cliffs, N.J.: Prentice-Hall, Inc., 1976.

Brazelton, T.B. *Infants and mothers: differences in development*. New York: Dell Publishing Co., Inc., 1969.

Cherry, C. *Creative play for the developing child*. Belmont, Calif.: Fearon Publishers, Inc., 1976.

Corbin, C.B., *A textbook of motor development* (2nd ed.). Dubuque, Iowa: Wm. C. Brown Co., Publishers, 1980.

Erikson, E. *Childhood and society* (2nd ed.). New York: W.W. Norton & Co., Inc., 1963.

Flavell, J.H. *The developmental psychology of Jean Piaget*. New York: D. Van Nostrand Co., 1963.

Fraiberg, S. *Every child's birthright: in defense of mothering*. New York: Basic Books, Inc., Publishers, 1977.

Frank L.K. *On the importance of infancy*. New York: Random House, Inc., 1966.

Gallahue, D.L. *Developmental play equipment for home and school*. New York: John Wiley & Sons, Inc., 1975.

Gallahue, D.L., Werner, P.H., and Luedre, G.C. *A conceptual approach to moving and learning*. New York: John Wiley & Sons, Inc., 1975.

Gerhardt, L.S. *Moving and learning: the young child orients himself in space*. Englewood Cliffs, N.J.: Prentice-Hall, Inc., 1973.

Kurtz, R., and Prestera, H. *The body reveals*. New York: Harper & Row, Publishers, Inc., 1977.

Levy, J. *The baby exercise book*. New York: Random House, Inc., 1973.

Ludington-Hoe, S. *How to have a smarter baby*. New York: Bantam Books, 1985.

McDiarmid, N.J., Peterson, M.A., and Sutherland, J.R. *Loving and learning: interacting with your child birth to three*. New York: Harcourt Brace Jovanovich, Inc., 1975.

Montagu, A. *Touching*. New York: Perennial, 1971.

Piaget, J. *The construction of reality in the child*. New York: Basic Books Inc., Publishers, 1954.

Piaget, J. *Play, dreams and imitation*. New York: W.W. Norton & Co., Inc., 1962.

Piaget, J. *The child and reality: problems of genetic psychology*. New York: Penguin Books, 1976.

Popper, A. *Parents book for the toddler years*. New York: Ballantine Books, 1986.

Robeck, M.C. *Infants and children; their development and learning*. New York: McGraw-Hill, Inc., 1978.

Sherrod, K., Vietze P., and Friedman, S. *Infancy*. Monterey, Calif.: Brooks/Cole Publishing Co., 1978.

Skinner, L. *Motor development in the preschool years*. Springfield, Ill.: Charles C Thomas, Publisher, 1979.

Stern, D. *The first relationship*. Cambridge, Mass.: Harvard University Press, 1977.

Werner, P., and Rini, L. *Perceptual-motor development equipment*. New York: John Wiley & Sons, Inc., 1976.

Werner, P.H., and Simmons, R.A. *Inexpensive physical education equipment for children*. Minneapolis: Burgess Publishing Co., 1976.

White, B.L. *The first three years of life*. Englewood Cliffs, N.J.: Prentice-Hall, Inc., 1975.

Index

OTHER TOYS 'N THINGS PRESS PUBLICATIONS

All Season Fun & Frolic — Indoor and outdoor activities for toddlers to school age.

Basic Guide to Family Day Care Record Keeping — Clear instructions on keeping necessary family day care business records.

Calendar-Keeper — Activities, family day care record keeping, recipes and more. Updated annually. Most popular publication in the field.

Family Day Care Tax Workbook — Updated every year, latest step-by-step information on forms, depreciation, etc.

For You, For Them — Trainer bibliography of audio-visual and print resources in 6 topic areas.

Forms Kit for Directors — Over 150 reproducible forms covering every need in an early childhood program.

Kids Encyclopedia of Things to Make and Do — Nearly 2,000 art and craft projects for children aged 4-10.

Open the Door, Let's Explore — Full of fun, inexpensive neighborhood walks and field trips designed to help young children.

S.O.S. Kit for Directors — Offers range of brainstormed solutions to everyday questions and problems.

Sharing in the Caring — Packets with family day care parent brochure, contracts and hints.

Staff Orientation in Early Childhood Programs — Complete manual for orienting new staff on all program areas.

Survival Kit for Early Childhood Directors — Solutions, implementation steps and results to handling difficulties with children, staff, parents.

Teachables From Trashables — Step-by-step guide to making over 50 fun toys from recycled household junk.

Teachables II — Similar to above; with another 75-plus toys.

Those Mean Nasty Dirty Downright Disgusting but... Invisible Germs — A delightful story that reinforces for children the benefits of frequent hand washing.